W9-AOV-843

Jubilee CELEBRATIONS

#1

Dorothy M. Harnish

Brethren Press

Copyright © 1994 by Brethren Press, a program of the Church of the Brethren General Board, 1451 Dundee Ave., Elgin, IL 60120

All rights reserved. The publisher of this book hereby grants permission to any congregation that uses it to reproduce portions of this book, including images, provided that no part of such reproduction is sold or distributed beyond services held in the local church and provided that proper credit is given to the original author. Where indicated, users must request permission to reprint from the original copyright holder.

The development of *Jubilee Celebrations 1* was made possible through a grant from Schowalter Foundation, Inc., Newton, Kansas.

This publication uses the New Revised Standard Version of the Bible, copyright © 1989, by the Division of Christian Education of the National Council of Churches of Christ in the U.S.A. Used by permission.

Cover design by Merrill Miller

98 97 96 95 94   5 4 3 2 1

Harnish, Dorothy M., 1941-
    Jubilee celebrations / Dorothy M. Harnish.
        p.   cm.
    Includes bibliographical references.
    ISBN 0-87178-477-7 (pbk. : v. 1)
    1. Worship programs. I. Title.
BV198.H37   1994   93-43573
264—dc20

Printed in the United States of America

Contents

The Spirit of the Lord is upon me,
because he has anointed me
to bring good news to the poor.
He has sent me to proclaim release to the captives
and recovery of sight to the blind,
to let the oppressed go free,
to proclaim the year of the Lord's favor.

—Luke 4:18-19

Preface

In my lifetime I have seen a small but steady stream of faithful churchgoers migrating between high and low liturgical denominations. Weary of a liturgical routine that no longer has meaning, the high church discontents seek out the simplicity of the low church. Longing for a deeper spiritual life, the low church discontents head for the high church and its encounters with the great mysteries of faith. We long for both depth and breadth in the church, yet our churches usually seem better at one than the other.

Jubilee Celebrations 1 bridges these gaps in our church experience. It brings together all kinds of expressions of faith into single events that fulfill many of our religious desires. It obscures the differences between worship and education, believing that each should contain the other. The celebrations are learning events that are worshipful and worship events that are educational. It works in at least three directions at once, providing opportunity for relationship with God, relationship with the church community, and a chance for mission to the world.

These celebrations are for the whole church. They are not just for children during the Sunday school, nor for adults during worship. On the day they are to be used, churchgoers are required to forgo their usual practice of dividing the congregation by age and again by function (worship and education). On this day the pastor, the education committee, and the worship committee combine their efforts in a whole new experience, the celebration.

Published as a companion to *Jubilee: God's Good News* (Anabaptist Curriculum Publishing Council, Box 347, Newton, KS 67114, 1994), this book is appropriate for any church that is willing to disband its usual Sunday morning program on occasion and try something new for an hour or two. Churches that are looking for midweek or Sunday evening programs or weekend retreats will also find plentiful resources in *Jubilee Celebrations 1.*

Five of the eight celebrations in this book feature special events in the church calendar: the opening of the church year, Thanksgiving, the Nativity, Lent, and Pentecost. Three celebrations are topical: the family, sabbath, and peace. Two of the eight celebrations, Simchat Torah and Sabbath, are reenactments of biblical festivals, providing the setting for and leading participants through traditional activities that have been practiced through the ages. It is not likely that any congregation will use all eight celebrations in one year. In fact, we presume that this is a resource that will aid your church for several years to come. And we expect that you will vary the plans as you need to. Feel free to use portions of it to enrich your regular worship or Christian education time.

Our world is fragmented and, sadly, the church is not often the place to find unity in a broken world. *Jubilee Celebrations 1* is a valuable resource that nourishes the whole Christian and the whole church, unifying varieties of gifts, services, and activities in the same Spirit. That is true cause to celebrate.

—Julie Garber
Editor

Introduction

How to use this book

These celebrations are for the whole church and require cooperation between pastors, worship committees, and education committees. The first item of business is to set up a meeting of key people from each group to plan a celebration. Then use the following list as an agenda.

1. Pick a date for your celebration and begin planning at least eight weeks ahead.

2. Plan for a 1½- to 2-hour time period to celebrate. Dispense with the regular worship time and Sunday school time. The celebration will accomplish both. Allow 30-45 minutes in each celebration for activities.

3. Modify. These celebrations were written for the typical church with a sanctuary, fellowship hall, and classrooms, an active Sunday school, and a multi-talented membership. If this doesn't describe your congregation, modify the plan to fit your people and facilities.

4. Activities are designed for school-age children through adults. Provide your usual care for preschoolers, infants, and toddlers.

5. Permission is granted, unless indicated otherwise, to reproduce prayers, litanies, and music in worship bulletins, provided that no part of such reproduction is sold or distributed beyond the event held in the local church and provided that proper credit is given to the original author.

6. If suggested hymns are unfamiliar, replace them with hymns from your congregation's hymnal or songbooks.

7. Invite guest speakers early to avoid schedule conflicts, and allow them plenty of time to prepare.

8. Assign leaders, musicians, and teachers in advance. They will need time to gather supplies, rehearse, and prepare presentations. Materials for activities are too numerous to include in the "You will need" section. Urge activity leaders to read their instructions early and gather all necessary items, remembering that in many cases participants will come to the activity centers in shifts.

9. To help you prepare, a sample bulletin is provided in each celebration. You may wish to include information that is specific to your event, such as hymn choices and locations of activity centers.

10. Brief instructions for activities are included in each celebration. Leaders may need to expand activities or try them out ahead of time to ensure smooth sailing on the day of the celebration. In very large congregations, duplicate activity centers to accommodate more people in small groups. Be prepared to direct people to the location of each activity center.

11. Several celebrations suggest a topic for a sermon or homily. The pastor may use the suggested topic or create a new one. Or the planning committee may decide to use an alternative to the sermon, such as a videotape or drama.

12. Promote the celebration four weeks ahead of time on posters and in church newsletters, bulletins, the newspaper religion section, and Sunday school handouts.

13. Many of the music resources suggested in *Jubilee Celebrations 1* are found in *Hymnal: A Worship Book*. The hymnal can be ordered from either Brethren Press (1451 Dundee Avenue, Elgin, IL 60120, 800 441-3712), Faith and Life Press (Box 347, Newton KS, 67114-0347, 800 743-2484), or Mennonite Publishing House (616 Walnut Avenue, Scottdale, PA 15683-1999, 800 245-7894).

The options for use of *Jubilee* celebrations are unlimited. Some congregations will find that Sunday evening worship, retreats, midweek services, or holiday programs are more appropriate times for *Jubilee* celebrations. Planning committees may wish to use portions of these celebrations for other occasions, and variation is possible and encouraged. Whatever form a celebration takes, it should uphold the philosophy of *Jubilee Celebrations,* whose intent is to unify children and adults, worship and nurture.

About the author

Dorothy Harnish is a staff member of the Congregational Resource Center sponsored by the Lancaster Conference of the Mennonite Church, Lancaster, Pennsylvania. She is a lifelong educator and innovator in the field of worship.

Celebrating the Book
Simchat Torah

A festival for the opening of the church school year

When my sister and I were little, we'd have bedtime devotions, read from the big, beautiful, children's picture Bible. "More, more," we would beg our mother. We wanted just one more story about Joseph or Moses or any one of the other fascinating characters in the Book.

Joy was part of our experience with the Bible. And the next day we could go to school with the assurance that God would be with us in what, to children, seemed all too difficult a world. We had the Joy of the Book—*Simchat Torah.*

—Cynthia D. Sautter

In the temple of Jesus' day, a portion of the Torah (the first five books of the Old Testament) was read aloud at each worship. It took one full year to read the entire Torah. Just as the readers were coming to the conclusion of Deuteronomy, the people would hold a festival to celebrate the end of one cycle of reading and the beginning of a new one with Genesis. This joyous festival for the love of the Bible is called Simchat Torah.

The Simchat Torah festival takes place on the last day of Sukkoth, also known as the Festival of Booths or Tabernacles. It begins at dusk and continues through the night with the final readings from Deuteronomy. By the end of the festival, the rabbi is beginning the new year with readings from Genesis. The rabbi takes the Torah scrolls out of their sacred place, the ark. He gives each scroll to a man and a great parade begins around the synagogue. Children participate in this celebration more than any other synagogue worship. They join in carrying and waving festive branches. Some carry flags with symbols on them, topped with the apple and candle representing the fruit and light of the

Word. And adults lift small children onto their shoulders to participate happily in the parade. Signifying the mandatory public reading of the Torah every seven years (Deut. 31:9-13), everyone processes around the synagogue seven times with exuberant singing and dancing. Each time around, different members of the congregation take turns carrying the scrolls, as the people reach out to touch or kiss the Torah scrolls. After all the singing and celebrating, they have many good things to eat. The next morning there is another procession to mark the end of Deuteronomy, followed by a reading from Genesis 1 to begin the year-long cycle again.

Modern celebrations of Simchat Torah include a blessing of the children. The children gather under a *tallit* (a prayer shawl) and an adult recites a blessing. Then an adult pronounces a benediction slowly so the children can repeat each line, thus joining in the

privilege of pronouncing the benediction. Still, in Israel today on Simchat Torah eve, the streets are filled with people dancing and singing far into the night.

Bible Scope
Nehemiah 8:1-12

Bible Text
Psalm 119:105

Bible Background for Our Festival

For many years the Israelites, overrun by their neighbors and stripped of their political power, lived in exile in Babylonia. They lived in misery, separated from the temple in Jerusalem, the place where God dwelled. Then the Persian King Cyrus let the Israelites return to their beloved Jerusalem. When the temple was partially rebuilt, the priest Ezra came back to Jerusalem with the Torah, placing these first five books of the Bible back in their rightful place. Nehemiah 8:1-12 records that sometime after Ezra's return, Simchat Torah, meaning the joy of the law, became the celebration of the people's love for the Book.

Jesus participated in Simchat Torah, which was held during the Festival of Booths at harvest time. Still today the Jews celebrate their love for the Torah with food, dancing, singing, and worship. And each year as Christians begin the church school year anew, when we give Bibles to children, or when we simply want to express our joy in the Book, we can celebrate Simchat Torah.

Faith Nugget
We celebrate the Bible because the Bible is our guide to all truth.

Early Preparation

Celebration of Simchat Torah is appropriate for a variety of special occasions in the church: as a rally day service to begin the church school year, for presenting Bibles to children, or to celebrate the whole church year. It is also a great opportunity to combine a junior high/youth lock-in with an all night reading of the Torah (Genesis to Deuteronomy) aloud, continuously, from the pulpit. Simchat Torah is also appropriate for launching short-term study courses such as "How to Study the Bible" or "How We Got Our Bible," or it may be used to initiate a read-through-the-Bible program or a Bible distribution project.

If you choose to reenact the festival during a regular worship time, involve everyone in the preparation.

Plan to welcome people on the day of the festival with a large banner that says Simchat Torah: the joy of the Book. On that day, hang it outside over the church door. Make the banner resemble a scroll by recycling an old vinyl window shade. Attach the ends of the shade to two wooden poles that are cut slightly longer than the ends of the shade. Or make several large Simchat Torah flags in advance (see p. 4 for instructions). Put one of the flags outside, then place one inside the entrance, one in the foyer, and one in the sanctuary. You will use these later in a procession during worship.

For an additional visual welcome, plan to display a collection of Bibles in various translations provided by members of the congregation. Include a Hebrew Bible and a Greek translation if you can find them. If you plan to launch a mission project during the festival, include a Bible in the language of the people you plan to serve.

As you prepare the bulletin for this festival, consider these specific suggestions: inside draw an open scroll for a border, placing the order of worship "on" the scroll; reprint the basic information about Simchat Torah (see p. 1) on a separate pullout sheet; if there is room on the pullout, include a special story for the children about the Bible, some Bible trivia questions, or a word search (see pp. 9-10).

You will need

❏ a Simchat Torah banner

❏ recorded or live Jewish liturgical music

❏ a collection of Bibles

❏ flag standards

❏ flashlights, lanterns, or candles

❏ a festival bulletin

❏ musicians, dancers, worship leader, pastor, readers

❏ leaders and materials for each activity center

❏ children's storyteller

Name of your church
Celebrating the Book
Simchat Torah

Getting Ready

Opening Prayer

Activities

1. Scrolls—Prepare replicas of the five scrolls of the Torah: Genesis, Exodus, Leviticus, Numbers, and Deuteronomy.

2. Flags—Make flags to carry in the procession and for the parade in worship.

3. Choir—Form a small intergenerational choir to learn the processional song, "Lamp of Our Feet," and the Simchat Torah celebration song for the parade.

4. Instrumental Music—Practice processional and parade songs with instruments such as the recorder, flute, trumpet, or homemade instruments.

5. Dance—Incorporate traditional Hebrew liturgical dance forms such as the hora or other circle dances during the processional and recessional.

6. Missions—Learn about Bible translation and distribution today.

7. Blessings/Benediction—In the Bible a benediction means putting good (*bene*) words (*diction*) on one another to send each other forth.

8. Sending Forth—Talk about the meaning of giving a parting blessing and be-
come comfortable with the process. In this joyful celebration we will emphasize the sweetness of the Word and the centrality of the Word in worship.

9. Scripture—Go quietly to the sanctuary to read Scripture.

Reenacting the Festival

Gathering Music

Words of Welcome

Call to Worship ..... "Good News Music"

Processional......... "Lamp of Our Feet"

Prayer

Hymn of Praise and Thanksgiving for the Bible

Offering

Children's Story .... "Golden Drops of Honey"

The Parade

Response

Blessing of the Children

Benediction

Sending Forth

Recessional

The Festival

A festival in Jesus' time was like our religious festivals today. The people made many preparations, such as baking special foods, making decorations, and reading the Torah before the actual event. As part of the festival today, the congregations will take part both in getting ready and in reenacting the festival.

Getting Ready

As people gather in the sanctuary or fellowship hall, welcome them with lively Jewish liturgical music (recorded or with live musicians, singers, and dancers). Musicians need not prepare more than one selection. Repetition will enhance the power of the selection.

Assemble for an opening prayer, the definition of Simchat Torah, and instructions for going to the activity centers. The Simchat Torah celebration will be more meaningful if everyone helps in the preparation. Group leaders, prepared in advance, will help participants carry out each activity that will be used during the worship. Younger children will enjoy participating in an activity with a parent. The goal is to mix the generations. Except where some skill is required, let everyone select a group. If time permits, participants may move on to more than one activity.

Activities

1. Scrolls. Using sticks, ribbon, and paper tablecloths or butcher paper, make the five scrolls for the parade. Roll up the scrolls and tie them with ribbon. Put the name of the book in large letters on the outside: Genesis, Exodus, Leviticus, Numbers, and Deuteronomy.

2. Flags. Each flag bears a Hebrew letter or a symbol of the Bible on it, and flag poles are often topped with an apple and candle signifying the fruit and light of the Torah. Core each end of the apple about one inch or 2.5 centimeters.

Set the apple on the top of the flag pole, and set a small candle in the top of the apple. Symbols for the flag include a tablet, crown, star of David, Bible words, scroll, menorah (candelabra), chalice, root of Jesse, or grapes. If you make 22 flags, have each picture a letter of the Hebrew alphabet as found in Psalm 119 of the New International Version of the Bible. Psalm 119 is a song that praises God's law. It is arranged as an acrostic. There are 22 stanzas, one for each letter of the Hebrew alphabet, with each line in a stanza beginning with the same Hebrew letter. Or you may wish to make 26 flags, using letters and symbols suggested in the Simchat Torah song.

3. Choir. Learn "Lamp of Our Feet" (p. 12) for the processional song and the Simchat Torah song (p. 11) for the parade.

4. Instrumental Music. To prepare for the processional and parade, practice "Lamp of Our Feet" and the Simchat Torah song with instruments such as the recorder, flute, and trumpet, or make instruments that will lend an air of spontaneity and engage the gift of children. Make shakers by putting a few dried beans in a can, use empty oatmeal boxes for drums, and place waxed paper over a comb and hum. Use your imagination to turn household items into instruments.

5. Dance. You may want to assign people to this group in advance to make sure both men and women and boys and girls of all ages are involved in learning the hora, a traditional Jewish liturgical dance. Let this be the final rehearsal. (See page 9 for instructions.)

6. Missions. To learn about the Bible today, what scholars are saying about it and who is translating it, invite a missionary or denominational resource person or a Bible teacher for a short presentation, or obtain one of many rent-free videos from the American Bible Society, P.O. Box 5656, Grand Central Station, New York, NY 10164, 800 543-8000.

7. Blessings/Benediction. The Simchat Torah ends with a special blessing by the children. This group needs children primarily and a few adults. If a prayer shawl is not available as a canopy during worship, a bed coverlet with fringe works well. Four adults, one at each corner, will hold the shawl over the heads of the children as an adult pronounces the blessing. Choose one adult to practice and read the blessing printed in the worship section. Have remaining adults choose favorite verses from Psalm 119 that they will use to bless the children and the congregation. Let the children practice reciting the benediction (Num. 6:24-26), repeating each phrase after the leader:

The Lord bless you, and keep you;
(children repeat)

the Lord make his face to shine upon you, and be gracious to you;
(children repeat)

the Lord lift up his countenance upon you,
(children repeat)

and give you peace. Amen.
(children repeat)

8. Sending Forth. Here are four suggestions for sending the worshipers forth joyfully.

a. Brief several children on how to help the minister send people out by having them dip crackers in honey as a reminder of the sweetness of the Word.

b. Have children make greeting cards with memory verses on them to hand out at the end of worship.

c. Prepare several children to send forth worshipers by stamping their hand with a rubber stamp. If available use a Bible message or appropriate symbol. If you cannot find such rubber stamps locally, you can order stamps of Psalm 34:8 and other verses from Purple Pomegranate Productions, 80 Page Street, San Francisco, CA 94102-5914, 415 864-3995. Or you may choose your own verse and have a local printer manufacture an inexpensive stamp. If none of these options are feasible, use any stamp—animals, happy faces, or sayings—to remind people of the Book.

d. Write Bible verses on narrow strips of paper that are long enough to encircle a wrist. During the Sending Forth, put a band around the wrist of each person and secure with tape or a staple.

9. Scripture. Choose people of various ages to read for 30 minutes from Deuteronomy. Ahead of time, listen to a recording of that portion of the Bible, or read it aloud in order to estimate where to begin so that the recitation concludes at worship time near the end of the book of Deuteronomy, preferably with chapter 32 or 33. Consider having the readers dress in Old Testament costumes. For additional visual effectiveness, have readers read from a large scroll of Deuteronomy, made by photocopying the last chapters of the book, taping them on butcher paper, and rolling the paper on two dowels. This group will not necessarily read during worship, but they will get a chance to experience the way in which the Scriptures were read continuously during Simchat Torah.

Reenacting the Festival

Gathering Music
Repeat the live or recorded Jewish liturgical music used for the opening.

Words of Welcome
The pastor or lay person gives a brief welcome and teaches about the origins and meaning of the Simchat Torah as found on pages 1-2 in the introduction.

Call to Worship
Have the leader read the poem "Good News Music" (p. 6), leading out with finger snapping and toe tapping. To increase the joyfulness and exuberance of

this poem, have the leader instruct the congregation to join in.

Processional

After an organ or piano introduction, the processional party begins to make its way up the aisle. Entering from the front door of the church, the choir and musicians performing "Lamp of Our Feet" are led by two people carrying the banner and flag carriers with flags prepared in the hour before worship. Children are intermingled. When they reach the front, the flag bearers plant their flags in standards or makeshift standards such as umbrella stands. Encourage musicians to keep up a lively pace and the flag bearers, especially children, to use graceful, energetic movements, including dancing and skipping. If the room is darkened, participants could carry lanterns, flashlights, and candles to create a festive mood.

Prayer

The worship leader offers a prayer of thanksgiving for the Book, ending with Psalm 119:103-106.

Our God, we invite you into this place today and come before you with thanksgiving for the gift of the Book that reveals who you are and what your will is for us.

Good News Music

How long will we come before the Lord
    with tired spirits and droning voices?
How long will we sit in half-filled churches
    and sing praise with noiseless songs?
How long will we worship with bored faces
    and dulled senses
    and offer tin when we could give gold?
Do we or do we not believe the news is good?

O Lord, you love us!
    Why aren't we shouting?
We don't have to earn it!
    Why aren't we singing?
The stone's rolled away!
    Why aren't we dancing
      to your good news music?

O Lord, you love us!
    Why aren't the bells pealing?
The victory's won!
    Why aren't the drums beating?
And you forgave us!
    Why aren't the harps resounding
      to your good news music?

Why aren't the feet stomping
    and the doves flying
    and the bands marching
    and the fingers snapping
    and the tongues praising
    and the hands clapping
    and the trumpets blaring
    and the choirs singing
    and the cymbals clashing
    and the children
      laughing?

And why aren't the people
    coming
      to
        bow
          down?

Why aren't the eyes smiling
    and the knees kneeling
    and the banners blowing
    and the horns sounding
    and the voices calling
    and the crowds clamoring
    and the arms waving
    and the tambourines playing
    and the hearts humming
    and the old men
      running?

And why aren't we
    crowning
      Christ
        Lord
          of
            Lords?

If the news is good . . .
    Sing!

(Reprinted from Reaching for Rainbows *by Ann Weems. Copyright © 1980 The Westminster Press. Used by permission of Westminster/John Knox Press. This poem may not be reprinted without written permission from Westminster/John Knox Press.)*

How sweet are your words to my taste,
  sweeter than honey to my mouth!
Through your precepts I get understanding;
  therefore I hate every false way.

Your word is a lamp to my feet
  and a light to my path.
I have sworn an oath and confirmed it,
  to observe your righteous ordinances.

Hymn of Praise and Thanksgiving for the Bible

All sing "Lord, I Have Made Thy Word."

Alternate selections:
"We Are Covenant People" (Mona Bagasao-Crane) *or* "The God of Abraham Praise."

Offering

Children's Story

The storyteller calls children to the front and tells them:

Today we are having a festival to celebrate the Bible. The festival is called Simchat Torah *(sim-hot tor-a).* **Say Simchat Torah with me. It means "The joy of the Book." Jesus celebrated Simchat Torah when he was a child and so did all of his ancestors. The people had a parade and took turns reading the Bible day and night. Learning to read was very important because when children could read they could help read the Bible for the festival."**

The storyteller then reads or tells "Golden Drops of Honey."

Ahead of time, copy some Hebrew letters on poster board and put a blob of honey on each one. Teach one child the letters before the festival. Let that child demonstrate how Aaron was rewarded for knowing his Hebrew letters so he could read Scripture. When the child identifies the letters correctly, he or she gets to eat the honey off the card with their finger. If time allows, tell other short stories from the Bible, such as the story of Jesus in the temple at age twelve or the call of the little boy Samuel studying the Torah with Eli.

The Parade

Have the Scripture reader, singers, flag bearers, dancers, and instrumentalists take their places at the front of the sanctuary. Hand out the scrolls randomly to people in the congregation. When everyone is in place and the congregation is quiet, the reader reads Deuteronomy 34 aloud. A second reader reads Genesis 1:1—2:3. The worship leader asks everyone who is able to parade around the sanctuary seven times, signifying the public reading of the Torah every seven years as mandated in Deuteronomy. As people stand, the organist or other musicians will begin playing an introduction to the joyous Simchat Torah song on page 11. When the choir begins to sing, the people begin parading. If the words are printed in the worship bulletin, the congregation can sing along. Other familiar songs could be sung during the parade such as "Down in My Heart," "Amen," "Jacob's Ladder," "B-I-B-L-E," or "This Is the Day." Dancers may join the

---

Golden Drops of Honey

Every day Aaron studied hard to learn his letters because he wanted to be able to read the Torah. His father told him that the Torah was special because it told of God's special rules.

His teacher, the rabbi, had a tablet with all the Hebrew letters written on it. There was a little dot of honey on each letter. The teacher told Aaron the honey was to remind him that God's rules are good and sweet just like the honey.

The rabbi would read a letter; then Aaron would say the name of the letter. If he answered correctly, he could eat the sticky, sweet honey with his finger.

Aaron could hardly wait! Today his family would celebrate the Festival of Shavuot. Always before, his brother and father would read the words in the Torah. Today he would be asked to read from the Torah too.

(By Mary Gene Morris Lee. From FESTIVAL: Worship with Jesus Today, VBS 1992, Ages 3-4, Student. Copyright © 1991 by Cokesbury. Used by permission. This story may not be reprinted without permission from Cokesbury.)

parade or perform the hora at the front. Adults can hoist little ones on their shoulders and let them feel the rejoicing! When flag bearers and scroll carriers have circled the sanctuary once, they may hand off their flag or scroll to another.

Response

When the parade is completed, the pastor asks everyone to be seated and calls for witnesses to the Word. At this time, people are invited to tell of a time when the Word of God was especially meaningful or to recite by memory favorite Bible verses. Be sure to give children an opportunity to share what they know or have experienced.

Blessing of the Children

You may want to form several groups for this blessing. To bless the children, gather them under a prayer shawl. Have parents surround the shawl, holding it up by its corners. Parents read or recite their favorite verses from Psalm 119, followed by a parent giving the blessing.

Blessed art thou, O Lord our God, King of the Universe, who has commanded us to teach our children about you. Bless them now as they stand in your presence covered by the blessing of our prayers. We offer them to you today, praying that they will grow up with the eyes of their minds alert and eager to study your Word. May the ears of their hearts always listen to your instructions.

May our suggestions, loving discipline, and example always direct them to you.

We offer this prayer in Jesus' name, your Word to us. Amen.

Benediction

After the blessing of the children, give the Numbers 6:24-26 benediction to the congregation. An adult, youth, or older child should say one phrase at a time, which the children then repeat. If they wish, children may raise their right hands in a prayerlike gesture of "putting on" good words.

**The Lord bless you, and keep you;
the Lord make his face to shine upon you,
and be gracious to you;
the Lord lift up his countenance upon you,
and give you peace. Amen.**

(Num. 6:24-26)

Sending Forth

The pastor gathers the children to help send everyone forth with honey and crackers, greeting cards, a Bible verse or symbol stamped on their hand, or a Bible verse on their wrist.

Recessional

The pastor and worship leader process out with flags while instrumentalists play "Lamp of Our Feet" or other appropriate postlude, or the people may go out in silence.

Hora instructions

The hora has six basic steps that are repeated over and over.
The dancers stand side by side, forming a circle by putting their hands
on each other's shoulders or holding hands. Then in unison, each dancer
(1) steps to the right with the right foot, (2) places the left foot behind
the right foot, (3) steps right with the right foot, (4) hops on the right
foot, (5) steps left with the left foot, and (6) hops on the left foot. As
these steps are repeated, each person will move one position to the right
each time.

Pullout sheet for the bulletin

Bible Trivia

1. The Bible is a collection of books. Can you name
    some of these?

2. What is the first book of the Bible? *(Genesis)*

3. What is the last book of the Bible? *(Revelation)*

4. Name the two parts of the Bible. *(Old Testament, New Testament)*

5. In which is the story of Jesus? *(New Testament)*

6. Which book in the Bible is a songbook? *(Psalms)*

7. Name a book of the Bible that is a letter from Paul to his friends
    in the church at Corinth. *(Corinthians)*

8. The stories of the Bible were first written in Hebrew and Greek.
    Did you know that the Bible has been translated into more
    than 240 languages today?

Bible Story

If you are the oldest child in your family, you may feel you have an
important job looking out for your brothers and sisters. They
look up to you. But in the Bible, the youngest child in the family is often the honored one. Read about Jacob and Esau (Gen.
27:1-29); David (1 Sam. 16:1-13); and the story of the two sons
(Luke 15:11-31).

Word Search

```
W A L C D O M W S I M C H A T
T O G E N E S I S R A H T X O
F R S T W R U I V A L E M I T
X L U K E Y C T T I V I T V N
B S Q B H S I D E T X J O H D
L W M A T T M E R W O Y G E
E U B A T W I D B A O H P E T
N P K R A M V O B M U N Q N E
T H S N M K E X O D U S O S G
I V I N G A L E V E Y R A M S
L X K M E V P T I R U S G X Y
```

GENESIS	NUMBERS	MARK
EXODUS	DEUTERONOMY	LUKE
LEVITICUS	MATTHEW	JOHN

Solution

```
W A L C D O M W S I M C H A T
T O G E N E S I S R A H T X O
F R S T W R U I V A L E M I T
X L U K E Y C T T I V I T V N
B S Q B H S I D E T X J O H D
L W M A T T M E R W O Y G E
E U B A T W I D B A O H P E T
N P K R A M V O B M U N Q N E
T H S N M K E X O D U S O S G
I V I N G A L E V E Y R A M S
L X K M E V P T I R U S G X Y
```

Simchat Torah Song

(Sing with energy and a quick tempo to the tune of "Are You Sleeping?")

Simchat Torah, Simchat Torah
Word of God, Word of God,
"A" is for the alphabet, "A" is for the alphabet
Praise the Lord, Praise the Lord.

"B" is for the Bible
"C" is for Creation
"D" is for King David
"E" is for the Exodus
"F" is for the first fruits
"G" is for the Gospels
"H" is for the Hebrews
"I" is for Isaac
"J" is for Jerusalem
"K" is for God's Kingdom
"L" is for the Lord's Day
"M" is for Messiah
"N" is for the New Moon
"O" is for our offerings

"P" is for the prophets
"Q" is for Queen Esther
"R" is for resurrection
"S" is for the sukkah
"T" is for the Torah
"U" is for the un-
   leavened bread
"V" is for the vineyard
"W" is for wandering,
   wandering in the wilderness
"X" stands for Christ
"Y" is for Yahweh
"Z" is for Mt. Zion

("Simchat Torah Song" by Martha Zimmerman from Celebrate the Feast, *© 1981, Bethany House Publishers. All rights reserved.)*

Lamp of our feet

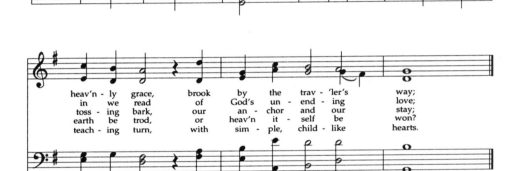

Lamp	of our feet,	where -	by we trace	our
bread	of our souls,	where -	on we feed,	true
pil -	lar of fire,	through	wat - ches dark,	or
word	of the ev -	er -	liv - ing God,	will
Lord,	grant us all	a -	right to learn	the

path when wont to	stray;	stream from the fount of
man - na from a -	bove,	our guide and chart, where -
ra - diant cloud by	day;	when waves would 'whelm our
of the glo - rious	Son;	with - out thee how could
wis - dom it im -	parts,	and to its heav - 'nly

heav'n - ly grace,	brook	by the trav - 'ler's	way;
in we read	of	God's un - end - ing	love;
toss - ing bark,	our	an - chor and our	stay;
earth be trod,	or	heav'n it - self be	won?
teach - ing turn,	with	sim - ple, child - like	hearts.

Text: Bernard Barton, *The Reliquary*, 1836
Music: Johan Crüger, *Praxis Pietatis Melica*, 5th ed., 1653

2

Celebrating Thanksgiving
Thinking and Thanking

A celebration of gratitude

> In Haiti neighbors share food, sending it in covered dishes carried by children. At young ages children imitate the customs of their parents, tearing off tiny portions of their two-cent pieces of cassava bread to share with friends.
>
> It is never polite to eat in the presence of others without offering some of your food. An unexpected guest who arrives when someone is eating may ask for some of the food without being considered rude. Haitians believe strongly that *manje kwit pa gen met*—cooked food has no owner.
>
> —*Joetta Handrich Schlabach*

Why is it that the less people have the more they share, and the more they must struggle the more grateful they are? Perhaps it is because hunger and poverty are constant reminders that life is fragile and that God is present in each morsel of food and scrap of clothing. Daily the poor remember the source of life and are grateful.

It is no coincidence that the linguistic root for the words *think* and *thank* are the same. Both are acts of gratitude. The first part of gratitude is remembering and thinking about God's goodness and grace. The second part of gratitude is thanking and praising God. Let this festival be a celebration of gratitude, helping those of us who take many things for granted reflect on and praise God, think and thank.

Many cultures observe this pattern of thinking and thanking during the harvest. Harvest festivals have taken place throughout history and around the globe. Three Jewish festivals (Passion, Passover, and Pentecost or Tabernacles) connect giving thanks to agricultural events. The first thanksgiving feast in the New World, attributed to the Pilgrims, carries strong Christian connections to the feast day of St. Martin on November 11, a day in medieval history that celebrated full barns and cellars with a church service, games, dances, processions, and a noonday feast of fatted goose and wine from the grape harvest. In England, Lammas Day on August 1 commemorated the harvest of grain with worship, feasting, and the consecration of loaves made from the first ripened grain. Puritan settlers did not retain these particular feasts, but in 1621 the Plymouth colony held a day of thanksgiving, which over time took on traditions such as praying, feasting, and playing games.

Bible Scope

Psalm 100; 2 Corinthians 9:15; Ephesians 5:20; Philippians 4:8

Bible Text

Psalm 100

Bible Background for Our Celebration

Thanksgiving is a supremely important religious discipline that we learn from the time we are small. However, Thanksgiving is not a holy day that is included in the liturgical year, perhaps because giving thanks is a constant activity that cannot be confined to a single day. Without realizing it, many of us remember Psalm 100, a song of thanksgiving, from childhood and can recite it by heart, just as the Hebrews must have recited it over and over. Psalm 100 is also a processional song that would have been sung as the people entered the gates to the temple. Embedded in this short psalm of thanksgiving is a creed or confession of faith that recalls why we are thankful. We give thanks because the Lord is God, we are God's people, and God is good. This summary statement sounds simple enough until we remember that the Jews were able to proclaim these fundamental truths even in the face of competing religions that threatened to overtake them.

Many beliefs and values compete for our loyalty today. When we are enticed to divide our loyalties between Christianity and other beliefs, we would do well to remember or think about God who delivers us and whose children we are and give thanks with this psalm.

How then shall the Christian community keep this day? Usually at Thanksgiving we associate even our modest riches with God's blessing. But what about the poor? Are they not also blessed? Sometimes our affluence causes hardening of the attitudes and we forget that God cares for everyone. We must remember, especially on this day, that we are celebrating the way God sustains us all. Rich and poor alike can be thankful that God provides what we need, not what we want.

Faith Nugget

Thinking of God is part of thanking God.

Early Preparation

Churches in temperate or warm climates may choose to hold the games and picnic breakfast outdoors. If you choose to begin outdoors, adapt games for the lawn and plan to move tables and chairs outside for the meal. If you do not plan to use photographic slides in the celebration, you may want to consider staying outdoors for the whole celebration. Northerners will probably want to stay inside! Be sure to let people know in advance that casual dress is appropriate for this celebration.

Announce in the church newsletter several weeks ahead that foodstuffs will be collected for needy families during the celebration. Find out what the most pressing local needs are from the staff at your local food pantry or shelter, and

encourage church members to bring those items.

Prepare the bulletin on one side of a plain sheet of paper. If the information will not fit on one side, print the overflow on an insert. During the activity time, people will decorate the plain backs with expressions of thanksgiving during the activity time and distribute them for worship. Collect the bulletins after worship and arrange them in a collage on a bulletin board.

You will need

☐ musicians for the processional

☐ donuts, apples, pumpkins for games

☐ food for the breakfast

- ❏ *inside* pages of the celebration bulletin
- ❏ a site and wood for a bonfire (optional)
- ❏ seasonal decorations such as wheat, cornstalks, pumpkins, bowls of uncooked grains
- ❏ a cookbook that features global food issues

- ❏ worship leader, readers
- ❏ three people to prepare a Thanksgiving testimony for the Message
- ❏ hosts for each table
- ❏ streamers on wands and balloons
- ❏ leaders and materials for activity centers
- ❏ plans for a 12- to 24-hour fast for youth and adults (optional)

Name of your church

Celebrating Thanksgiving

Thinking and Thanking

Gathering

The Meal

Activities

1. Offering Bags—Decorate sturdy, recycled brown bags to receive thanksgiving offerings of nonperishable food items.
2. Pumpkin Decorations—Decorate pumpkins for the worship area.
3. Gratitude Tree—Make a gratitude tree to place at the altar or on the worship table.
4. Bulletins—Design bulletin covers for the worship time and a collage.
5. Music and Slides—Illustrate the hymn texts of harvest praise songs.
6. Signing—Learn the hand signs to "God Is So Good."
7. Fasting (optional)— Youth and adults fast for 12 to 24 hours.
8. Praying the Psalms—Pray the psalms of gratitude in a quiet place.
9. Dance—Create dance movements to Psalm 100.

Gathering Again

Call to Worship

Processional. . . . . "All People That on Earth Do Dwell"

Confession

Assurance of Pardon

Hymns

Children's Story . . . . "Pedro's Gift"

Offering

Offertory Response . . . "God Is So Good"

Message. . . . . . . "Thinking and Thanking"

Litany of Gratitude

Benediction

The Celebration

If space and weather permit, the out-of-doors is a natural setting for this celebration. And if your congregation is in a rural or camp setting, a bonfire would add warmth and serve as a worship center.

Gathering

Use the first few minutes of the celebration to gather everyone in the sanctuary or fellowship hall, and introduce the celebration and the events of the day. Since early harvest traditions included games, play a quick game of bobbing for donuts or apples hanging from strings, or have a pumpkin roll relay. For the relay, divide participants into teams of eight. Using only their heads, players roll a pumpkin 25-50 feet or 7-14 meters ahead, around a chair, and back to the base line, passing off the pumpkin to the next team member in the relay.

The Meal

In the church or around the bonfire, serve an informal and simple breakfast feast. Provide or have participants bring assorted breads. Supply drinks and toppings of butter, jams, and cheese spreads. Here is a suggested menu: corn muffins or cornbread with apple butter or jams, a fresh fruit tray or stewed hot apples, cheese chunks, hot and cold beverages. Use uncooked grains and cookbooks as a centerpiece on the food table. Assign a host to each table. Encourage the generations to spread out so that each table has a representation of children, youth, and adults. When everyone is served, read Meister Eckhart's words:

There is no such thing as "my" bread. All bread is ours and is given to me, to others through me, and to me through others. For not only bread but all things necessary for existence in this life are given on loan to us with others, and because of others and for others and to others through us.

(From Extending the Table, © 1991 Herald Press.)

Pray:

"Lord, to those who hunger, give bread. And to those who have bread, give the hunger for justice."

(From Extending the Table, © 1991 Herald Press)

Sing the Johnny Appleseed song and enjoy the bread feast.

Activities

After the meal, invite everyone to join in the celebration activities, taking part in as many activities as they have time for. Ahead of time assign locations for each activity and instruct participants where to go. Leaders of simple activities should plan for many participants in shifts. Leaders of more complicated or time-consuming activities may have the same group for the whole time.

1. Offering Bags. Decorate sturdy, recycled brown bags to receive thanksgiving offerings of nonperishable food items. Provide bits of fabric, felt, crayons, magic markers, construction paper, glue, stickers, various shapes of macaroni, or kernels of rice and corn to glue on. Before worship, place the open bags around the foot of the worship center or altar.

2. Pumpkin Decorations. Let each person decorate a small pumpkin or cut out and decorate a pumpkin of construction paper. Then ask participants to complete one of the following sentences and write it on their pumpkin with a black marker: "I am thankful for . . ." or "A hard thing I want to be thankful for in my life is . . ." Just before worship, line the center aisle of the sanctuary or the path to the worship area with pumpkins.

3. Gratitude Tree. Anchor a tree branch in a bucket of sand. Cut out colored leaves from construction paper, letting adults help the younger children. Write "things I am thankful for" on each leaf. Using a hole punch, attach yarn to the leaves and hang them on the gratitude tree. Just before worship, add the gratitude tree to the items on the altar or worship table.

4. Bulletins. Let children and adults help decorate bulletin covers with crayons, stamps, and markers. Ask them to draw something that God provides for which they are grateful. Be sure they sign their work of art. If you have bulletin inserts, assemble the bulletins with the additional material that was prepared ahead of time, and distribute the bulletins as the people gather again for the worship. Bulletins could be collected after the celebration to be made into a collage.

5. Music and Slides. Illustrate the hymn texts of harvest praise songs (see p. 18 for suggestions) by choosing appropriate slides from a collection. Or have participants in this group, including children, make designs on write-on slides, which may be purchased from an education supply store. If slides are not available, let people draw on overhead transparencies with colored markers. Show these slides or transparencies to illustrate the thanksgiving hymns selected for worship.

6. Signing. Teach the hand signs to "God Is So Good" (p. 22). Let children and adults accompany the song with signs during worship. You may also have time to have the children create movements to "Day by Day" by Richard of Chichester (p. 21).

7. Fasting. Consider inviting youth and adults to fast 12 to 24 hours before the feast to heighten their awareness of the source of all food and increase their gratitude for God's grace. Fasters might want to stay in the church together overnight. With supervision, youth could make a 12-hour fast the focus of a lock-in or retreat that ends with the congregational celebration.

8. Praying the Psalms. Provide a quiet place where people can go to pray the psalms of gratitude such as 100, 107, and 136. If you are meeting in a camp or rural church, suggest that the group split in two to read antiphonally from opposing hilltops or across a field. Antiphonal reading can also be done in the sanctuary if it is unoccupied during the activity time.

9. Dance. People who like creative movement can put movement to Psalm 100 (see Call to Worship below). Let them accompany the reading of the psalm during the Call to Worship. It will be helpful for the dancers to meet with the readers to rehearse together sometime in the week preceding the celebration. Let the activity time be the last rehearsal.

Gathering Again

Allow time for people to bring their creations to the sanctuary or worship center and to place pumpkins along the aisle or path. Ask several people to move the cookbooks and bowls of grains from the food table to the worship center. As people enter, help children hand out the decorated bulletins.

Call to Worship

When people are seated, call them to worship with Psalm 100. Three readers, representing the oldest members of the congregation who have observed many harvests, will read the psalm. If there are dancers, they will accompany the reading.

Readers 1, 2, 3: Make a joyful noise to the Lord, all the earth.

Reader 1: Worship the Lord with gladness;

Reader 2: come into his presence with singing.

Reader 3: Know that the Lord is God.

Readers 1, 2: It is he that made us,

Reader 3: and we are his;

Reader 2: we are his people,

Reader 1: and the sheep of his pasture.

Readers 1, 2, 3: Enter his gates with thanksgiving,

Reader 1: and his courts with praise.

Reader 2: Give thanks to him,

Reader 1: *bless* his name,

Reader 2: bless *his* name,

Reader 3: bless his *name*,

Readers 1, 2, 3: *Bless His Name.*

Readers 1, 2: For the Lord is good; his steadfast love endures forever,

Reader 3: and his faithfulness to all generations.

Processional

Have the congregation sing "All People That on Earth Do Dwell." Instrumentalists (brass instruments, winds, or bright stringed instruments such as the banjo) lead the procession. Have the congregation join in singing as the children and youth process in, singing and carrying streamers on wands or balloons. Following the youth, the choir processes in as well. Once everyone is in, sing together another Thanksgiving hymn from your hymnal.

Confession

(unison)

**Remove far from me falsehood and lying;
give me neither poverty nor riches;
feed me with the food that I need,
or I shall be full, and deny you,
and say, "Who is the Lord?"
or I shall be poor, and steal,
and profane the name of my God.**

(Prov. 30:8-9)

Assurance of Pardon

Leader: Because of God's great love for you
and God's rich mercy for all,
you are fully forgiven.

People: We will live as those who are truly loved
and truly forgiven
through the gift of God's grace.

(Copyright © 1982 Mennonite Publishing House. Used by permission.)

Hymns

Sing two or three Thanksgiving hymns, using the slides made earlier to accompany each hymn. Possibilities include:

"Now Thank We All Our God"

"Praise to God, Immortal Praise"

"Come, Ye Thankful People"

"We Plow the Fields and Scatter"

"Sing to the Lord of Harvest"

"To God Be the Glory"

"Oh, for a Thousand Tongues to Sing"

Children's Story

Read "Pedro's Gift" (p. 19).

Offering

Thanksgiving calls for an offering of jubilation. Have the congregation stand and process to the worship center with their gifts as a musical offertory is played or the congregation sings. Try a tune that is upbeat and easy to sing without hymnals, such as the Johnny Appleseed song or "We Give Thee But Thine Own." Repeat as many times as needed. This is also the time for people to fill the decorated bags at the worship center with foodstuffs as well as bring their monetary offering.

Offertory Response

Children and adults respond to the offering by singing and signing the hymn "God Is So Good."

Message

Thinking and Thanking. The pastor or lay people give personal examples of remembering God's grace and thanking God. Very meaningful testimony might be provoked by the question, "What is the most difficult thing you are grateful for?"

Litany of Gratitude

As a litany the worship leader or pastor reads the messages on the pumpkins that line the aisle or path, with the congregation responding to each one by saying: "Thanks be to God for his indescribable gift!" (2 Cor. 9:15)

Benediction

Be filled with the Spirit, as you sing psalms and hymns and spiritual songs among yourselves, singing and making melody to the Lord in your hearts, giving thanks to God the Father at all times and for everything in the name of our Lord Jesus Christ.

(Eph. 5:18b-20)

Pedro's Gift

The last of the rice had been harvested. The men had threshed it with their bare feet and the wind blew the chaff away. It had been a good year with an abundant harvest. Pedro's father loaded his sacks of rice onto the Jeepney and took them home where he stored them in large baskets, hoping to keep the rats from getting into the rice. Rice was their main food for the coming year. He set one sack of rice aside.

Pedro came running into the house, calling, "Dad, can we cut down some banana stalks to decorate the church for the Thanksgiving service tomorrow? You should see how nice it looks already. There are bunches of coconuts, stalks of sugar cane, and baskets of fruit and vegetables already on the platform."

"Sure, son," answered his dad, "choose the ones with nice leaves, ones that the last typhoon didn't tear up."

On Thanksgiving Sunday morning Pedro's mother and other women from this church in the Philippines were up early preparing food for the dinner after church. Some of the men were barbecuing a whole pig over the open charcoal pit.

Pedro's family dressed for church. A Jeepney taxi came to get them. The family climbed in while Pedro's father loaded the sack of rice he had set aside. He called it "the Lord's rice." It was their Thanksgiving offering to God. Father turned to Pedro and asked, "Pedro, what is your offering to the Lord?"

Pedro was surprised and stammered, "Mine? Why, I didn't think I needed to bring anything. I'm just a child."

"But you have had a good year, Pedro," said his father. "God has given you good health and helped you in school, hasn't he?"

"Well, yes," Pedro replied slowly, "but what can I give God?"

"You have ten beautiful chickens, Pedro. You didn't lose even one this year," Father reminded him. Just then the driver of the Jeepney honked his horn. Pedro's father jumped in the taxi and away the family went, leaving Pedro standing by himself.

Pedro walked around to the back of their house where he kept his chickens. He looked thoughtfully at his ten white Leghorn chickens. He was proud of them. How could he give one away?

The Thanksgiving service was long but beautiful. Six babies were dedicated. The choir sang. The church was full. The missionary preached the sermon.

Then it was time for the offering when the worshipers took their gifts of money or produce to the altar. Pedro's father put the sack of rice by the Communion table. Pedro stood in the back. He carried a beautiful white chicken under his arm. He joined the others going forward. He knelt by the communion table and placed his chicken on the floor. Then he took the piece of twine that was tied around the feet of the chicken and tied the other end to the leg of the table. He gave the best he had to God who had given so much to him.

(From Children's Time in Worship *by Harriet Houston, copyright © 1981 Judson Press. Used by permission of Judson Press.)*

Day by Day

Day by day, dear Lord,
of Thee three things I pray:
To see Thee more clearly,
Love Thee more dearly,
Follow Thee more nearly,
Day by day.

—Richard of Chichester

God is so good

Text: Traditional
Music: Traditional African

God is so good. (repeat 3 times)

God is good to me.

God loves me so. (repeat 3 times)

God is good to me.

Jesus   died   for   me. (repeat 3 times)

Jesus   is   good   to   me.

I   will do   God's will. (repeat 3 times)

God   is   good   to   me.

Reprinted by permission from INCLUDING CHILDREN IN WORSHIP, Copyright © 1991 Augsburg Fortress. May not be reproduced further without written permission of Augsburg Fortress.

Celebrating the Nativity
God's Gift

A celebration of the incarnation of Christ in the church and in the world

We gathered around our Christmas tree. The grownups fell thankfully into favorite chairs and children plunked down close to the magic tree in that incredible position with knees bent and feet pushed behind them. Tiny hands impatiently fingered small gifts hanging on low branches, and bright-eyed glances and awed whispers told us they could barely wait.

"Wait!" I said to the eager ones. "Before the gifts, we will have our prayers, as we always do."

We began with the eldest in the group, and one by one each family member offered a special Christmas prayer. Then it was time for the prayers of the three youngest children.

Lisa said her prayer with an understanding far beyond her years. Then Lee, age 4, began. Now this little fellow never lacks for words. He prayed on and on. The others grew fidgety as he asked God to bless each family member by name. Then he invoked God's care upon as many countries the world over as he could remember.

The only one left in our circle to pray was Lauren, age 3. She looked at the bright star topping the tree and then at her mother. Tears began to roll down her cheeks. She did not know what to do. She had laryngitis and could not speak a word.

Lee patted her hand and looked up with big brown eyes: "Lauren can kneel!" he said.

Quickly Lauren scrambled to her knees and bent her little blonde head for a long time. Surely God heard that mute prayer in a special way!

I often think of that day, whenever words fail me. I know that I can always, like that little child, kneel!

—Faye Field

(Reprinted from JED Share, *Winter 1986, © 1986 by United Church Press. Used by permission.)*

The mystery of the incarnation has the power to touch us deeply and bring us to our knees. The wonder is not only that Jesus embodies the Word of God, but also that we as the church are the body of Christ. This is a great and humbling mystery! This celebration helps us learn about the incarnation. And as God gave us the Christ child, we in turn give our gifts.

Bible Scope
Luke 1; Matthew 2:1-12; John 1:1-5, 14

Bible Text
Luke 1:26-38

Bible Background for Our Celebration

The Gospels of Matthew, Luke, and John tell of the incarnation—the Word made flesh, God with us, Emmanuel. Mark is the only Gospel that makes no mention of Jesus' origins. In Matthew we have the story of the wise men who hear of the special baby and travel a long distance to see him. When they find him, they refuse to disclose the place to King Herod who fears his new rival. Luke tells the fullest story of Jesus' birth and the events leading up to it. In Luke 1:26-38, Mary hears the news that God will send a son and she will be the child's mother. John claims that the Word was with us from the beginning. Now the Word becomes flesh and dwells among us.

In response to the news of the incarnation, the wise men bring gifts and Mary gives of herself freely to help make God's will a reality. Likewise, the nativity story prompts us to ask ourselves how we can live in an incarnational way. How can we serve the cause of making God's will a reality in the world?

Faith Nugget

We freely offer ourselves up to help make God's will a reality.

Early Preparation

This celebration can be easy or complicated, depending on the planners' time and energy and whether you plan to have a live creche. If you plan to have a live nativity scene with people and animals, you will need to make arrangements well ahead to erect a shelter and schedule shifts of people to create the scene. Ask a farmer or the local zookeeper to lend trustworthy animals and to supervise the use of the animals. Let the community know through the religion section of the local newspaper that they may come to see the live creche and worship with you.

Plans call for families to bring nativity scenes to decorate windowsills and other spaces in the church. Be sure to put out a notice well ahead of time so families can bring their creche the week before the celebration.

Most congregations hold special services on Christmas Eve or Christmas Day, and many have an annual Christmas program featuring the children in the church. Consider using this celebration on one of those occasions and actively involving the whole congregation.

You will need

- ❑ enough index cards for each person attending to have one
- ❑ instrumentalists, carolers, storyteller, children for the tableau
- ❑ real or stuffed animals, bird/cage
- ❑ worship leader, song leader, readers of all ages
- ❑ rhythm instruments
- ❑ festival banner and lanterns or luminaries
- ❑ live Christmas tree (balled if possible)
- ❑ a raised platform for the stable
- ❑ a copy of *The Different Drummer* by Scott Peck
- ❑ costumes
- ❑ birthday cake
- ❑ leaders and supplies for the activity centers
- ❑ ½-inch candles for candlelighting (1 candle per person)
- ❑ a Christ candle

Name of your church

Celebrating the Nativity
God's Gift

Gathering

Call to Worship

Hymn . . . . "Joy to the World"

Caroling

Prayer of Confession

Prayer Response

The Christmas Story

Hymn . . . . "Away in a Manger"
(actors exit)

Hymn . . . . . . "Go Tell It on the Mountain"

Children's Story . . . . "Baboushka:
A Story from Russia"

Choral Response . . . . "My Gift"
"Little Drummer Boy"

Activities

Love Incarnate—(1) Make a gift of loving
service. (2) Or contribute to Heifer
Project International or similar
organization.

Hope Incarnate—(3) Make dream catchers.
(4) Or send homemade Christmas
cards to prisoners.

Peace Incarnate—(5) Make kits for Church
World Service. (6) Or make edible decorations for live tree and the birds.

Joy Incarnate—(7) Make musical instruments to give away. (8) Or make jump
ropes to jump for joy.

Gathering Again

The Message . . . . "The Rabbi's Gift"

Honoring the Word Made Flesh
with Our Gifts

Candlelighting

Benediction

The Celebration

Begin the celebration outside with a brass ensemble playing Christmas hymns or a group of carolers singing a capella at the entrance to the church. If the service is held at night, line the walk with luminaries or have the carolers hold lanterns. Off to the side have a cluster of shepherds and two adults and a child, in costume. If you are in a rural setting, add animals such as sheep, a cow, a donkey, and a large dog. If it is impossible to stage the tableau outdoors, have greeters meet people outside and invite them in to see the tableau in the narthex or foyer. Invite them to sing along with the carolers.

Inside, put candles or electric lights in the windows. Or plan ahead to invite different families to bring nativity scenes for each window, and illuminate them with votive candles. At the worship center, place an empty manger accented with light. Put the live Christmas tree at the front of the sanctuary, or use it as a prop in the nativity tableau.

Before worship begins, Mary and Joseph in costume will take seats with the congregation where most worshipers can easily see them (they may remove headdresses until they say their lines). Shepherds who were staged at the entrance now wait just outside the sanctuary, and wise men position themselves at the back of the church or in the balcony. Baby Jesus may stay with his or her family until the appropriate time. If using a doll, ask someone to hold it as if it were alive.

Gathering

After the congregation is seated in the sanctuary, carolers or choir come in from the rear of the sanctuary with the children's ensemble and instrumentalists, singing "O Come All Ye Faithful." The songleader should stand at the front and indicate to the congregation that they should stand and join in on the second and remaining verses.

Call to Worship

(led by an older child or youth)

One: The message of Christmas is this—Christ has come!

People: Christ has come!

One: The Word became flesh!

People: And dwells among the people.

One: The Word became Emmanuel!

All: Emmanuel, God is with us.

Hymn

"Joy to the World"

Pass out rhythm instruments such as drums, sticks, tone blocks, bells, triangles, maracas, and tambourines to enliven the hymn. Divide the congregation into two groups, and sing "Joy to the World" antiphonally.

Group 1: Joy to the world

Group 2: the Lord is come

Group 1: Let earth

Group 2: let earth

Group 1: receive

Group 2: receive

Group 1: her king

Group 2: her king

Group 1: Let every heart

Group 2: Prepare him room

Together: and heaven
and nature sing
and heaven
and nature sing
and heaven and heaven
and nature sing

Caroling

Let worshipers request favorite carols for the whole congregation to sing. Try the Moravian tradition where a child sings a phrase with an adult responding. In this case, let the congregation respond. If a child is too timid to lead, have an adult lead out. A favorite in this style is "Morning Star, O Cheering Sight" (p. 33). Sing all carols in unison if many worshipers cannot read music or are unfamiliar with the songs.

Prayer of Confession
(leader)

The Word became flesh and dwelled among us. But we had no room for the expectant family, no respect for the prophet in our midst. We did not even try to save you from persecution and eventually death.

We are like Mary—unworthy to help make God's will a reality, but eager to say yes. Let us rejoice in your invitation to us and help us to be your body, your heart, your hands in this world. Amen.

Prayer Response
(congregation in unison)

For God so loved the world that he gave his only Son, so that everyone who believes in him may not perish but have eternal life. Indeed, God did not send the Son into the world to condemn the world, but in order that the world might be saved through him.

(John 3:16-17)

The Christmas Story
Luke 1–2 and Matthew 2, page 30.

Hymn
"Go Tell It on the Mountain"

You may want the choir to perform this piece rather than singing it as a congregation.

Children's Story
Invite children to come forward to hear the story, "Baboushka: A Story from Russia" (p. 31). The storyteller can set the mood, saying, "It is Christmas Eve. The wind is blowing. It is very cold. Can you hear the wind? Perhaps as you hear the story of Baboushka you will be reminded of someone else."

Read or tell the story. Without moralizing, ask children what they would like to say about the story. Whatever they offer, let it be. Ask as if to oneself, "I wonder who Baboushka reminds us of?" Whatever is contributed, let it be. Thank the children and tell them to return to their seats. "Barrington Bunny" is another appropriate story that is available on film from EcuFilm (see Resources, p. 94).

Choral Response
A member of the children's or adult choir recites Christina Rossetti's poem, "My Gift," and the choir sings "The Little Drummer Boy."

My Gift

What can I give Him
Poor as I am;
If I were a shepherd,
I would give Him a lamb,
If I were a wise man,
I would do my part,
But what can I give Him?
I will give my heart.

—Christina Rossetti

Activities
To reinforce the concept of incarnation, that God's love was made real, the congregation will exchange names and move to activity centers to make gifts for each other that are symbolic of the incarnation. Love, joy, peace, and hope are made into real objects and given to church friends as a reminder that the Word made flesh dwells among us.

Have everyone take an index card from the pew rack and write his or her name on it. If an offering is taken, collect the cards at this time, and redistribute the names down the row. Instruct people where to go to make their gift, and allow time for everyone to make one gift and bring it back to the sanctuary.

1. Love incarnate. Give the gift of loving service to the person whose name you drew. Decorate small cardboard jewelry boxes or other small containers to look like the wise men's vessels. Cover the container with bits of torn masking tape, and stain with a little shoe polish to look like leather. Inside, put a coupon with a promise to do some job, such as raking leaves, washing windows, preparing food; or use your talents to write a song, a poem, or create a piece of art.

2. Love incarnate. Collect your loose change (or more) to contribute to Heifer Project International (P.O. Box 808, Little Rock, AR 72203), an organization that provides livestock, bees, chicks, rabbits, fish, and goats to needy people around the world. As a group decide which animals you will buy. It takes very little money to buy a chick or hive of bees. Make a card for the person whose name you have drawn, saying that a contribution has been made in his or her name in order for love to become real to our world neighbors. Write to Heifer Project for order information.

The Christmas Story

Luke 1—2 and Matthew 2

As readers of all ages read the Christmas story from Scripture at a microphone, actors playing the parts of Gabriel, Mary, Joseph, Jesus, the shepherds, and wise men will enter, making their way to the stable raised in a front corner of the sanctuary. A bird in a cage or a large, well-behaved dog will add to the scene. If the celebration is at night, darken the sanctuary and use a spotlight to follow actors from their entrance to the stable.

Scene 1

7- or 8-year-old reads Luke 1:1-38, the Annunciation.

Mary enters with Gabriel, who is carrying a dove in a cage. Mary sits down near the center aisle at the front, preferably on steps leading to the worship table so she can be seen. Gabriel hovers over her. They freeze in place.

Scene 2

9- or 10-year-old reads Luke 1:46-56, the Magnificat.

The angel gives Mary the birdcage and moves off stage. Mary unfreezes and responds to the news. She may then dance and freeze or take a position of praising God.

Scene 3

11- or 12-year-old reads Luke 2:1-5, the journey to Bethlehem.

Joseph enters and joins Mary. Together they move from one side of the stage to the stable raised in the corner and freeze.

Scene 4

A youth reads Luke 2:6-7, the birth of Jesus.

Gabriel returns to "deliver" the doll or real child who represents Jesus. He hands the child to Mary and Joseph.

Scene 5

A young adult reads Luke 2:8-14, the shepherd scene.

The shepherds take positions in the corner at the other side of the sanctuary. The spotlight focuses on the shepherds and their dog, cowering and looking at the angel in amazement (standing slightly above at the other side of the sanctuary). They freeze.

Scene 6

An adult reads Luke 2:15-20, the shepherds at the stable.

The shepherds unfreeze and rush to the stable to see Jesus. They and the angel take positions next to Mary and Joseph and freeze.

Scene 7

An older adult reads Matthew 2:7-12, the story of the wise men.

The wise men bearing gifts also enter from the other side of the sanctuary or from the middle aisle and walk regally to the stable. They kneel before the baby and freeze. The creche is complete.

Hymn

While the creche figures are still posed, the congregation sings "Away in a Manger" a capella.

Exit

As the actors in the Christmas story exit, have someone with a dramatic voice read the following scriptures:

(as the wise men exit a different way than the way they came) And having been warned in a dream not to return to Herod, they left for their own country by another road.

(Matthew 2:12)

(as the shepherds and angel leave in a hurry) The shepherds returned, glorifying and praising God for all they had heard and seen, as it had been told them.

(Luke 2:20)

(as the holy family leaves) The child grew and became strong, filled with wisdom; and the favor of God was upon him.

(Luke 2:40)

3. Hope incarnate. Make dream catchers by melting crayon shavings between 4-inch or 10-centemeter circles of waxed paper by pressing with an iron, or use markers on white paper and wipe with salad oil. Give the dream catcher to the person whose name you drew to hang in a sunny window as a reminder that hope in Jesus Christ is real.

4. Hope incarnate. Send homemade Christmas cards to prisoners. Make up two cards with your greeting and sign your name on one card. Give the second card to the person whose name you drew, providing them with a stamped and addressed envelope. Contact your denominational office for names and addresses of prisoners who would like to receive cards.

5. Peace incarnate. Ahead of time, find out from Church World Service (475 Riverside Drive, New York, NY 10115, 212 870-2257) how to make a health kit, sewing kit, or school kit for someone in another country. Assemble the kits and lay them under the tree at the close of the celebration. Give the person whose name you drew a little card that says: A kit has been given in your name.

6. Peace incarnate. For environmental peace and harmony, make edible decorations for the live Christmas tree in the sanctuary—edible for the birds, that is! Stuff pinecones with peanut butter; string popcorn and cranberries; melt suet and add cracked corn or bird seed, letting the mixture harden in half shells of oranges or grapefruits or molding it inside an onion bag. Attach string for

Baboushka: A Story from Russia

The fire crackled. The wind roared. There was a sudden knocking on the door.

"Who's there? Who's there?" cackled Baboushka from her rocking chair.

"We are shepherds from the hills come to tell the happy news."

"What is it? What is it before I lose my patience?"

"On this happy, happy morn in Bethlehem the king is born. Come with us to worship him in Bethlehem."

"I will, I will. But not until I sweep the floor, clean the cupboards, scrub the door. I will, I will!"

"Baboushka, Baboushka, the baby cries for you."

"I will come . . . tomorrow. Tomorrow will do!"

There was nothing more that they could say, and so the shepherds went their way.

The sun shone. The flowers bloomed. There was a tapping at the door.

"Who's there? Who's there?" groaned Baboushka from her rocking chair.

"We are the wise men from the East come to tell the happy news."

"What is it? What is it before I lose my patience?"

We have seen his star above and come to find the king to bring to him our gifts of love. Come with us, Baboushka dear, for the king is very near."

"I will. I will. But not until I bake a plumcake for the king and make the child a covering."

"Baboushka, Baboushka, the child waits for you."

"I will come . . . tomorrow. Tomorrow will do."

There was nothing more that they could say and so the wise men went their way.

When the house was spotless, the cupboards clean, and not a speck of dust was to be seen, when the cake was baked and the covering made, Baboushka packed her presents all, now to search for the stable and the stall.

But when she got there, the stable was bare, and empty was the stall.

Through town and country, night and day, Baboushka wandered on her way, seeking, seeking, seeking.

So on each Christmas Eve you may see sneaking up the stair a little wrinkled lady leaving her gifts there for every girl and boy to celebrate the joy of Jesus' birth, because Baboushka knows . . . tomorrow may be too late.

What are the gifts the lady brings? Time to wonder, time to sing, hands to help, a loving heart . . . gifts suitable for a king.

(Retold by Elaine Ward in Being with God: Advent Devotions. *Copyright © 1988 Educational Ministries. Reprinted with permission.)*

hanging the ornaments. Give the ornament to the person whose name you drew, and let him or her put it on the tree at the end of the celebration. Following the celebration, take the tree outside or contribute it to a community place, such as a retirement home, park, or nursery school.

7. Joy incarnate. Make musical instruments, using waxed paper and combs for kazoos, beans and cardboard containers for maracas, jugs filled with water for a jug band, or heavy paper plates and can lids for tambourines. Be creative with containers, sandpaper, blocks of wood, and other things found around the house. Give the instrument to the person whose name you drew. He or she can use it in the last part of the celebration to express joy.

8. Joy incarnate. Make jump ropes to encourage jumping for joy! This is a good gift for adults to make for children. Fill two or three dishpans with fabric dye. Have people cut 6- to 8-foot or 2- to 2.5-meter lengths of cotton clothesline. Tie knots in the rope 6 inches or 15 centimeters from each end and fray the ends. Dip the jump rope in the dye and set dye according to directions. Wring out excess liquid.

When people have finished their gifts, they may take a piece of Jesus' birthday cake. Cut the cake when enough people have gathered to sing a rousing chorus of "Happy Birthday."

Gathering Again

Have everyone return to the sanctuary or fellowship hall and give their gift to the person whose name they drew. Then ask everyone to be seated.

The Message

Select someone in advance to read "The Rabbi's Gift," found on pages 13-15 in *The Different Drummer* by Scott Peck.

Honoring the Word Made Flesh with Our Gifts

Recognizing there is a little bit of Christ in everyone, we give our gifts as a symbol of God with us. As the congregation sings "Angels We Have Heard on High" or "Hark the Herald Angels Sing," people with bird feed ornaments should place them on the live tree and people with kits should place them under the tree. People with homemade instruments may play them during this joyous carol.

Candlelighting

Begin by having several people carry light from the Christ candle to the four corners of the sanctuary and light the candles of people at the ends of each row. They in turn pass the flame down the row. Have a music leader hum "Lo, How a Rose E'er Blooming," encouraging the congregation to join in while the candles are being lighted. When candles are lighted, sing "Joy to the World" or "Silent Night" as a congregation. Lift candles a little higher on each verse. If your church does not allow candlelighting due to danger of fire, consider using flashlights or a large group of candles on the worship table. Have one or two adults light the candles.

Benediction

The light shines in the darkness, and the darkness did not overcome it. Amen.

Morning Star, O cheering sight!

Text: Johann Scheffler, 1657; tr. Bennet Harey Jr., 1885
Music: Francis F. Hagen, 1836

Celebrating Lent
The Discipline of Lavish Giving

A celebration of devotion

One Sunday, returning home from church, I was having the typical what-did-you-do-in-Sunday-school-today conversation with my two sons. The younger, who was six, came up with this: "My teacher, we made bread together and I ate mine already and it was good." My son had learned that the people of the Bible made bread themselves and that making bread was important for their life together. He had also learned, through his own experience, that he would make bread with people at church and that it was good. He had "played" with the people of the Bible, "played" with his teacher and his classmates, "played" with bread, and "played" with the images that bring all these together. He ate it all and found it was good.

—Craig Dykstra

As soon as Easter became a weekly festival (in the form of the eucharist), the early church began to observe a time of preparation. By the Council of Nicea in A.D. 325, Easter lasted forty days each year, extending from Ash Wednesday to Easter Eve. It was a time of spiritual cleansing, which included self-deprivation to remind people of Jesus' forty days in the wilderness as a time of preparation for his life's ministry. Similarly for us, Lent is a time of deliberate self-deprivation, not so much as repentance for our sins but as a way to unclutter our lives in preparation for what God is calling us to do. It is a time to offer ourselves lavishly to God, giving with childlike abandon and knowing that unrestrained devotion to God is good.

Bible Scope

Matthew 26:6-13; Mark 14:3-9; Luke 7:36-50; Psalm 15

Bible Text

Matthew 26:6-13

Bible Background for Our Celebration

This is a story of extravagant love poured out in response to the compassion of Jesus. It takes place shortly before the passion drama unfolds as Jesus prepares the disciples for life without him.

Our English translations say that the woman anointed Jesus with ointment from an alabaster jar. Throughout Jewish historical and biblical writings, anointing was a powerful action, used often to bring kings to the throne. And Jesus was a king, of sorts. But the word used here for anointing, *aleipho*, is different. It means "to pour out." The motivation for anointing Jesus is not to give him power but to give him a kindness. The woman poured out kindness in appreciation for Jesus.

Jesus received the anointing as a gift. He too needed to receive love, lavish love given with abandon that did not stop to count the cost of being misunderstood.

The disciples who watch the anointing react the way we think Jesus should have; they criticize the woman for being wasteful and said she should have sold the expensive oil and given the money to the poor. And Jesus reacts almost as we think the disciples might have. His reply surprises us in two ways. First he commends the woman's generosity when he usually encourages frugality, and then he seemingly brushes off the poor whom he usually defends. Why this strange reaction? Think of this scene as an anointing for Jesus' death, a death that will bring something even greater than money to the poor. As promised in the Sermon on the Mount, they will inherit the kingdom of God. The poor, who will be with us always, are blessed, not forsaken. They are heirs of the kingdom, which will partially be fulfilled through the death and resurrection of Christ. The anointing serves the twofold purpose of preparing Jesus for death and fulfilling the scriptural promise of inheritance.

No matter how we resolve this curious situation in our minds, this text is finally about loving Jesus. He declared the woman's act a beautiful thing. It was not only a good act (*agothos*) but a lovely act (*kalos*). This passage pushes us to accept the fact that in the kingdom of God extravagance is not wasteful in the same way that the last shall be first. The woman gives us permission to be lavish in our love for Jesus.

Faith Nugget

Lenten disciplines steer us away from preoccupation with self, toward total and lavish love of God.

Early Preparation

As your committee plans a date for the Lenten celebration, consider holding the celebration on the fourth Sunday of Lent, which some churches consider a week of refreshment or breaking the fast.

Ahead of time, create a visual center for the celebration by draping deep purple cloth over the worship table or altar and arranging extravagant objects on it. Include the cross to represent Jesus' extravagant sacrifice for us.

You will also need to prepare printed explanations ahead of time about the significance of the pretzel for Lent (p. 46). These will be handed out with pretzels as people leave the worship place.

You will need

❑ extravagant objects: perfume decanter, model of an expensive car, cross, string of imitation pearls, a brick painted gold, jewelry box, forced flower bulbs

❑ purple cloth

❑ musicians, dramatists, storyteller(s)

❑ perfumed oil for anointing

❑ twisted pretzels with explanation

❑ people to anoint others

❑ purple lapel ribbons and straight pins for every member

❑ leaders and materials for activity centers

❑ a copy of *Gift of the Magi* by O. Henry to retell to children

❑ a slide of Dürer's "Praying Hands"

Celebrating Lent
The Discipline of Lavish Giving

Gathering

Call to Worship. . . . . St. Teresa's Prayer

A Story. . . . . "Gnarled Hands"

Pastoral Prayer

The Lord's Prayer

Hymn. . . . . "Take My Life"

Children's Story. . . . . *Gift of the Magi*

Anthem . . . . "Praise God from Whom
All Blessings Flow"

Scripture Dramatized . . . Matthew 26:6-13

Message

Hymn

Lavish-Giving Activities

1. Buy One, Give One Free—Challenge each other to buy two *quality* items and give one away.

2. A People Fast—Encourage one another to participate in nonfood fasts.

3. If I Had a Million Dollars—Talk about how you would spend a million dollars on *someone else.*

4. Guided Prayer—Have someone lead the group in quiet contemplation.

5. Feetwashing, the Modern Way—Discuss ways of volunteering time for others.

6. Story Swap—Tell personal stories of frugality and discuss ways to be extravagant.

7. Youth Potlatch—Practice outdoing each other in gift-giving.

8. Toys Are You—Children, with adult assistance, make Jacob's Ladder for others (K-5th grades).

9. Posters—Junior high youth make posters for the Great Commandment.

10. Prayer List—Provide for people on a prayer concerns list.

Gathering Again

Offering

Litany of Response

Anointing

Benediction

Going Out

The Celebration

Purple is the symbol of both royalty (extravagance) and penitence (self-denial). It is the perfect color for Lent when we deny ourselves the usual pleasures in order to give ourselves wholly and lavishly to God.

Gathering

As people arrive at the celebration, greet them with a bulletin and a purple lapel ribbon and a straight pin. As people enter they will also see the worship center draped in purple, displaying some extravagant objects. Consider using purple on windowsills, on the lectern and pulpit, and on banners. You may want to explain in the church newsletter about the use of purple during Lent and encourage people to wear purple clothing to the celebration.

Call to Worship

Christ has no Body now but yours
No hands, no feet on earth but yours
Yours are the eyes through which He looks
Compassion on this world
Yours are the feet with which He walks
To do good

Yours are the hands with which He blesses
All the world
Yours are the hands
Yours are the feet

Gnarled Hands

Young Albert straightened his back and stood up, then hurried away from the bench where he had been working. He glanced at his hands and sighed. They had grown a little rough from helping his father in the goldsmith shop. He thought of the canvas in his room with its half-finished painting. He wanted to paint more than anything. But there were so many mouths to feed and so little money for art lessons.

"Father . . ." Albert began, his words sticking in his throat. "Father, I—I want to leave home and become an artist. I know you can't help me with money for art lessons but if I work . . ." He lowered his eyes. This was harder to talk about than he'd thought.

His father looked up from his workbench. "Then put your tools away, Albert. I'll help what little I can."

Without a word Albert cleaned off the bench and walked into his room and packed his clothes. He was excited, yet sad. He knew he had to go to the city to study with a great artist, but first he had to find a job so he could pay for his rent and food.

His father shoved a few bills into his hand. "Here, Albert. It's all I can spare."

Several days later Albert boarded a train. It rumbled and lurched along the winding tracks until it reached the city. His heart hammered as he thought, *Soon I will study with this great artist and become a good painter.* His bit of money was soon gone, but finally he found a job. He had to work during the day and study art at night. The working and studying wore him out. Many times after a hard day's work he fought sleep as he studied, and it was hard to keep his mind on painting.

One day he came to know a kind, older man who also studied with the artist.

"Why don't you move in with me?" the man suggested. "We'll both save money that way."

After Albert moved in with the older man in the shabby attic, he hoped things would go easier. But it was still hard, because both worked during the day and studied at night. Sometimes Albert was so tired he was ready to tumble into bed when he came home from work. How could he ever become an artist this way?

"This won't work, Albert," his friend said one day, shaking his gray head. "We're not getting anywhere. Maybe one of us ought to work to earn the money we need while the other one spends all his time studying art. Then when the paintings begin to sell, the other one will have a chance at art."

Albert nodded. "All right. I'll work and you'll study. I'm younger and stronger, so earning our keep is up to me."

"No, no!" his friend cried. "I already have a job which pays enough to take care of us both. Besides, you've got more talent than I. Don't waste your years working so that an old man can learn to paint!"

Yours are the eyes
You are His Body

Christ has no Body now but yours
No hands, no feet on earth but yours
Yours are the eyes through which He looks
Compassion on this world
Christ has no Body now on earth but yours

—*Teresa of Avila*

(Translated by John Michael Talbot. Copyright © 1986 BMG Songs, Inc. All rights reserved. Used by permission. This poem may not be reprinted without permission of BMG Songs, Inc.)

A Story

Arrange for a storyteller to present "Gnarled Hands" by Esther L. Vogt. Introduce the story by saying:

Today we are celebrating Lent. Although we usually think of Lent as a time of self-sacrifice and deprivation before Easter, Lent is actually a time of preparation for Easter when we avoid anything that sidetracks our devotion to God.

The emphasis is on our devotion, not on our sacrifice. We are so accustomed, however, to making sacrifices at Lent that the thought of being extravagant in our love for God and each other seems inconsistent.

In our celebration today we are going to practice extravagant and outrageous kindness. First listen to this story about extraordinary kindness.

(Note: If a slide of Dürer's "Praying Hands" is available from your library or college, project the praying hands on a screen for everyone to see.)

Pastoral Prayer

Loving Lord, our sacrifice of coffee, sweets, bad habits, and credit cards during Lent is not enough. These are merely the small things that keep us from loving you in a big way. Help us understand this season of Lent as a season of

---

Albert realized his friend meant it, and he dug into his studies with enthusiasm while his friend scrubbed floors and washed dishes in a café. Albert hated to see him looking so tired at night but the old man refused to give it up.

"The harder I work in learning how to paint, the sooner my friend will have his chance," Albert decided.

No matter how gray the day or how tired he was, his friend whistled cheerfully, because he believed some day Albert would be a great artist!

One day Albert sold a wood carving. Rushing back to the apartment, he threw the money on the table.

"Here!" he shouted. "Now it's my turn to be the breadwinner. I earned enough money from my wood carving to pay for food and rent for a long time. And it's time for you to study art again."

His eyes blurring with happy tears, the old man quit his job at the café. He set up his easel and began to daub paints and oils on a canvas, working long and hard. Then he threw down his brush and wept. He found he couldn't paint anymore!

Something had happened. His fingers had grown gnarled and twisted, his arms stiff, and his joints enlarged—all from the hard work. He knew he could never paint again. He tried to keep Albert from finding out, but Albert soon noticed his friend's sadness.

"What's the matter, friend?" he asked anxiously.

"Look!" The old man stretched out his worn, calloused fingers. "I guess I've worked so hard that I can never use my brushes right again . . ." His voice faded away.

Albert caught his breath sharply. *Why he's sacrificed himself because of me,* he thought. *And I can never give him back what he gave up so I could become an artist.* He remembered a verse in the Bible that talks about "workmen that need not be ashamed." *That's my friend, all right,* Albert thought, with a lump in his throat. *But how can I ever make it up to him, God?* he prayed.

One day when Albert came home to the apartment, he found the old man seated at the table with his head bowed, the rough, twisted hands folded reverently in prayer.

I know! An idea popped into Albert's mind. *I'll make a picture of those hands as they are folded in prayer. Then the whole world will see the hands of this kind, unselfish man who sacrificed so much for me to become an artist. In spite of the broken fingernails and swollen joints, those are the most beautiful hands I've ever seen!*

And so Albert (Albrecht) Dürer portrayed the hands of his friend for every girl and boy, man and woman to see. And he called the picture simply: PRAYING HANDS.

(By Esther L. Vogt. Used by permission.)

extravagance and lavishness for you. Let us forsake the distractions in our lives, such as competition, self-centeredness, false piety, and gratification, that leave no time for true devotion. We pray for boundless energy to serve you, nourishment to serve others, discipline for our faith, and complete abandon in our love for you.

The Lord's Prayer
(in unison)

Hymn
"Take My Life"

Children's Story
Gift of the Magi by O. Henry (retell in language children can understand)

Anthem
"Praise God from Whom All Blessings Flow" (pp. 47-49)

Scripture Dramatized
Dramatize Matthew 26:6-13. Decide whether to use a Bible times setting or a contemporary setting. Have a narrator read the Bible Background from a lectern or pulpit or from center stage, then move off to the side to narrate the scripture. As the text is read, actors pantomime the story. Or make a script from the text and let actors say their own lines.

Message
Pastor or lay speaker connects this story to Lent and Jesus' lavish gift to us.

Hymn
"Lord, with Devotion We Pray" *or* "Joyful, Joyful, We Adore Thee" *or* other hymn of praise

Lavish-Giving Activities
Since we are well trained in being frugal, we need to exercise the impulse to be extravagant for God and for each other. Let everyone choose one group that meets for 30 minutes to practice being extravagant. Give instructions for moving into groups.

1. Buy One, Give One Free. This group is for people who like to give bulk or generic food to the food bank and old clothes to the resale shop, but haven't considered buying something new or nice to give away. The leader should bring in a sack full of cast-off clothing. Pass it around and have people imagine where they would wear the clothes. Comment on their condition. Try to put together a whole outfit—pants and shirt or skirt and blouse. Talk about what the participants usually give to relief and what they would be willing to share. Then challenge each other to buy double on their next shopping trip and give one away. If they buy quality canned goods for their family, but generic for the food bank, they should consider buying two quality items and give one away. When they are buying summer outfits for the kids, they should buy an extra and give it to someone who needs it, or give it to Goodwill or the Salvation Army. Set a date when the group will bring their items to church and package them for the clothing store or food pantry.

2. A People Fast. Talk about the biblical concept of fasting as a spiritual discipline. For help, see Richard Foster's book *Celebration of Discipline.* The leader's guide to the book suggests nonfood fasts. After all, for most of us, food is not what distracts us from our practice of prayer and devotion. Foster suggests fasting from people. "Until we have learned to be alone, we cannot be with people in a way that will help them, for we will bring to that relationship our own scatteredness." Find partners who can encourage one another through the week to abstain from media, the telephone, and advertisements. Work together to make a list of ways to express devotion during the people fast.

3. "If I Had a Million Dollars . . ." As a group, answer this question, If I had a million dollars, how would I spend it . . . on someone else? Keep track of the ideas generated and give them to the church board. These suggestions may help them know how to use outreach money to help others. Most of us don't have a million dollars but we do have more than we need. As a group, brainstorm ways to make aid money go farther.

4. Guided Prayer. Let someone skilled in leading prayer guide others in quiet contemplation. The leader may say:

Remember . . .

—a time you received a lavish gift of love poured out.

—a time you gave a gift and the giving was a source of joy to you.

—a time you received an expression of lavish love that involved risk for the giver.

—a time you risked in order to give more lavishly.

The leader may ask:

What does the text for today call you to do?

Does it call you to let go of the control?

Does it ask you to experience anointing or to anoint someone else with kindness?

Does it ask you to risk pouring out love and kindness?

Who is God calling you to anoint with kindness?

5. Feetwashing the Modern Way. Washing a guest's feet was a great kindness and a symbol of great personal sacrifice in Bible times. In a circle, with dishpans and towels, take turns washing each other's feet until each one has washed another's feet and had their own feet washed. Think of a modern equivalent, such as duty in a soup kitchen or shelter. Invite someone from Habitat for Humanity or another group to talk about the organization's work. Generate interest in joining in as volunteers.

6. Story Swap. Since we are more accustomed to being frugal than being lavish, we all have stories about how cheap we or our parents are. Let each person in the group complete this sentence: "My family is so cheap that to us _____ is an extravagance." Suggest that partici-

pants indulge soon in the extravagance they have just mentioned, and challenge them to double their offering one week this month.

7. Youth Potlatch. Read about the potlatch of Native North Americans of the Pacific Northwest. The potlatch was a celebration in which groups tried to outdo each other in giving. Divide the participants in this activity into two teams. Send one team off to decide on a gift for the other team, such as breakfast in bed at a retreat. The gifts should start small and be priceless, literally! They should also be things that are actually possible. Come back together for the presentation. The second team goes off to decide on an even better gift for the first team. Go around three or four times. Then talk about having a retreat in which these gifts are actually delivered.

8. Toys Are You. Have kids from kindergarten or first grade through fourth or fifth grade make Jacob's Ladders with the help of adults (p. 45). Make it clear that the toys will be collected at the end of the celebration to give to needy children. If you have enough material, allow children to make a second one for themselves.

9. Posters. For junior high-age children, emphasize that love of God and neighbors requires all we've got. Make posters using the first part of the great commandment, "Love the Lord your God with all your heart, soul, and mind." Trying making the posters without words, using only pictures for words. Or have groups of kids work on parts of the verse, putting their posters together at the end of the period for the complete verse and then posting them so others can guess the verse. Large groups can try additional verses such as Micah 6:8, "[All that is required of you is] to do justice, and to love kindness, and to walk humbly with your God."

10. Prayer List. Ahead of time, contact your pastor for a list of congregational members who need prayer support. Shower the people on the prayer concern list with love in the form of cards, meals, transportation, and childcare, or whatever is needed. Write cards and organize needed assistance during the activity period.

Gathering Again

Call the people to return to worship. Sing hymns of praise such as "I Will Praise the Lord," "To God Be the Glory," and "Praise, I Will Praise You, Lord."

Offering

Having just practiced being extravagant, challenge people to give generously, even lavishly. Recite 2 Corinthians 9:7: "God loves a cheerful giver."

Litany of Response

Leader:
O Eternal Wisdom, O Vulnerable God,
  we praise you and give you thanks,
    because you laid aside your power
      as a garment
    and took upon you the form of a slave.

People:
You became obedient unto death,
    even death on a cross,
    receiving authority and comfort
    from the hands of a woman;
  for God chose what is weak in the world
    to shame the strong,
  and God chose what is low and
    despised in the world,
    to bring to nothing things that are.

All:
Therefore, with the woman
    who gave you birth,
    the women who befriended you
    and fed you,
    the woman who anointed you
    for death,
    the women who met you,
    risen from the dead,
  we praise you.

Leader:
Blessed is our brother Jesus,
  who on this night, before Passover,
  rose from supper, laid aside his
    garments,
  took a towel and poured water,
  and washed his disciples' feet,

saying to them:
"If I, your Lord and Teacher,
  have washed your feet,
  you also ought to wash one
    another's feet.
If you know these things,
  blessed are you if you do them.
If I do not wash you,
  you have no part in me."

People:
Lord, not my feet only
  but also my hands and my head.

All:
Come now, tender Spirit of our God,
  wash us and make us one body in
    Christ;
  that, as we are bound together
  in this gesture of love,
  we may no longer be in bondage
  to the principalities and powers
    that enslave creation,
  but may know your liberating peace
  such as the world cannot give.
    AMEN

(By Janet Morley. Adapted from All Desires Known, *Second Edition. Copyright © 1994, Morehouse Publishing. Used by permission.)*

Anointing
The pastor or lay leader says,

In remembrance of the woman who gave lavishly to Jesus and to prepare ourselves for extravagant love of God, we will anoint each other with sweet smelling oil this morning. Remember that the woman was not so much preparing Jesus for death as she was preparing him for his immeasurable sacrifice. Let the sweet smell remind us of Jesus' sacrifice and the sacrifices we can make in order to love more.

Send out one person to every two or three rows of the congregation with scented baby oil or scented anointing oil. He or she wipes the palm of the hand of the first person in the row and says, "These hands are anointed to be an instrument of God's lavish love" or another short blessing. That person, in turn, takes the bottle or vial and anoints the palm of the next person, and so on down the row.

In preparation for this activity, purchase a vial of oil-based essence available where air fresheners are sold. Put a few drops of the essence in a bottle of olive oil. Then make up several small amounts of oil using bottles with caps, such as aspirin bottles.

Benediction

When all have been anointed, the pastor or lay leader offers a benediction.

We who have been so generously forgiven, love much. Go in peace to be lavish and extravagant in your love of God and the body of Christ. Amen.

Going Out

As people leave the worship place, hand them a pretzel with an index card explaining the significance of the pretzel for Lent.

Jacob's Ladder

You will need six pieces of wood about the size of dominoes (1½ x 3½ x ¼ in. or 4 x 9 x 1 cm.) for each child. Have a carpenter in your congregation cut pieces of lattice to 3½ inches or cut the pieces from a two-by-four with a power saw. You will also need three ribbons for each child (¼ x 24 in. or 1 x 60 cm.).

Lay the blocks out in a row, end-to-end, keeping blocks about ¼ inch or 1 centimeter apart. With a pencil, number them 1 to 6, left to right. Use a power stapler to tack one ribbon to the end of block 1 in the very center.

Pass the ribbon over block 1 and tack it to the end of block 2.

This time pass the ribbon under block 2 and tack it to the end of block 3.

Pass the ribbon over block 3 and tack it to the end of block 4.

Pass the ribbon under block 4 and tack it to the end of block 5.

Pass the ribbon over block 5 and tack it to the end of block 6.

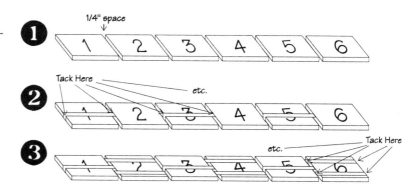

Clip off the excess ribbon. The other two ribbons run along either side of the center ribbon and weave over and under the blocks oppositely from the center ribbon. Start at the opposite end.

Tack the ribbons at the end of block 6.

Pass the ribbons over block 6 and tack to the end of block 5.

Pass the ribbons under block 5 and tack to the end of block 4.

Pass the ribbons over block 4 and tack to the end of block 3.

Pass the ribbons under block 3 and tack to the end of block 2.

Pass the ribbons over block 2 and tack to the end of block 1.

Clip off the excess ribbon.

Each block should have a staple in the center of one end and two staples at either side of the other end. Use a small tack hammer to tighten the staples. Ribbons should lie flat against the wood but not be too tight or too loose. Keep a distance of ¼ inch or 1 centimeter between blocks.

Hold the toy by the edges of the first block. Tip the block downward so it is back to back with block 2. Watch the blocks tumble!

The Significance of the Pretzel

Long ago, Christians kept a strict fast all through Lent. Even their bread had to give up some ingredients—no eggs, no butter. All that was left was flour, water, yeast and salt.

Long ago, when Christians prayed they folded their hands to themselves. They put their right hand on their left shoulder and their left hand on their right shoulder to form a cross. (And maybe to keep them from mischief so they could concentrate on prayer!) In Lent they twisted their bread into "little arms" crossed in prayer. These were called *bracellae* in Latin or pretzels in English. People gave pretzels to each other during Lent and that's the only time they ate them. They did this to help each other remember to keep the fast, pray diligently, and give money to the poor during Lent.

Praise God from whom

*Alternate phrases: Praise God from whom all blessings flow, praise God all creatures here below, praise God above, ye heav'nly host

Text: Thomas Ken, *Manual of Prayers for the Use of Scholars of Winchester College,*1695, altered 1709
Music: Boston Handel and Haydn Society Collection ..., 1830

*Alternate phrase: O praise our God, bless'd Three-in-One

Celebrating Pentecost
Happy Birthday to the Church

A celebration of the birth of the church

> *Come Holy Spirit, Heavenly Dove,*
> *With all thy quickening powers,*
> *Kindle a flame of sacred love,*
> *In these cold hearts of ours.*
> *Come shed abroad a Savior's love,*
> *and that shall kindle ours.*
>
> —Isaac Watts

Often today we feel no rushing winds, no tongues of fire in "these cold hearts of ours." Consequently, we long for the fire to be kindled in us. *Kindle*—what a beautiful word of the Spirit! Pentecost is the commemoration of the day the Spirit "ignited" the church, setting people on fire for faith, and it is a celebration of the Spirit that constantly rekindles our hearts with new energy to be the church and do God's will.

Bible Scope

Genesis 11; Acts 2

Bible Text

Acts 2

Bible Background for Our Celebration

According to the Acts 2 account, Jews were gathered in Jerusalem for *Shavuot*, a Jewish festival marking the end of Passover. (Originally a barley harvest, it was later referred to as law day in commemoration of Moses receiving the Ten Commandments.) At the same time, Luke tells us that the disciples were also in Jerusalem where Jesus, in an appearance, told them to wait for a baptism of the Spirit.

Several themes and images run through the Pentecost story. One is the theme of incarnation of the Spirit. This was not the first time the Spirit was manifest in the world. We first hear of the Spirit's activity in the story of creation. Then the Spirit appears again in the Gospels, baptizing Jesus for ministry. At Pentecost, the Holy Spirit appears a third time to empower the followers of Jesus to continue the work he began. With the Holy Spirit, the church is formed, twelve confused men are turned into powerful evangelists, and three thousand believers are added to the church.

Images of wind and fire are also important Pentecost elements. They are recurring images in the Bible that signal the presence of God and the Spirit. Wind is a symbol of life. In the Genesis account of creation, God breathes the breath of life into Adam and gives Adam spirit. Fire, representing God, leads the Hebrews out of Egypt (Exod. 13) and speaks to Moses but does not consume the burning bush (Exod. 3). The Spirit at

Pentecost brings life to the church, and the fire kindles a desire in us to be faithful.

One of the most interesting themes of the Pentecost is the theme of scattering. In Genesis 11, we have the story of the Tower of Babel. The people, fearful of being separated from one another, seek refuge in the tower to keep from being scattered. However, God wants the people to scatter, to take the message far and wide, so, as the story goes, he forces the people to speak different languages. Separated not by distance but by their inability to communicate, they are forced to scatter to take God's message abroad. In the story of the Pentecost, the opposite is happening. The scattered faithful come back together, and though they speak all different languages, they can understand each other perfectly. Unified in the church and baptized by the Spirit, they ask what they should do now. Having repented, they willingly devote themselves to a mission of teaching, enjoying fellowship, breaking bread, and praying.

As we celebrate the birthday of the church, we are actually celebrating the diversity of our far-flung community and our unity in one faith.

Faith Nugget

Followers of Jesus were taking the good news far and wide to every culture and language. Though they were far-flung, they were unified by the Holy Spirit. Though they spoke in tongues, they understood each other in the language of faith.

Early Preparation

If you just completed a major Easter celebration a little more than a month ago, your enthusiasm for another major production may be low. This Pentecost celebration is planned to minimize advance planning and the complexity of the event. Most props are readily available, the food is easy to prepare, and the dramatic portions are not complicated.

Musicians, dancers, and actors will need the most time to prepare. Give assignments to these people first. Also, contact your denominational headquarters to order information about your denomination's mission program (where your church is represented in the world, what kind of work is being done).

This Pentecost celebration is a celebration of unity in the midst of diversity. Every church is a living, breathing example of diversity. Reflect as a planning committee on the diversity of your congregation and the ways in which it is unified. The reflection will help you prepare for the celebration and create the right spirit.

You will need

- ❑ brochures from your denominational offices about service opportunities (use as bulletin inserts)
- ❑ cupcakes or sheet cakes and trick candles that don't go out
- ❑ worship center items (globe, maps, suitcases, passports, foreign language phrase book, Bible)
- ❑ drafting table, lectern, and tall stool
- ❑ sign that says "Upper Room"
- ❑ leaders and materials for activity centers
- ❑ birthday wrapping paper, ribbons, and balloons for the front door of the church
- ❑ party favors and noisemakers
- ❑ dancers
- ❑ flutists, banjo player

❑ youth to present dramatized reading of the scripture

❑ narrator and celebration leader

❑ powerful fan

❑ flashlights and plastic report covers

❑ clypping ribbon: red ribbon or red paper for paper chains

Your church name

Celebrating Pentecost
Happy Birthday to the Church

Gathering

Call to Worship

Hymn

Reading

Prayers

Hymn . . . . "God of Grace and God of Glory"

Dance . . . . "Spirit of the Living God"

Scripture

Activities

1. Bible Study on Wind and Fire—Discuss Bible stories about wind and fire, the Spirit at work.

2. Bible Study on Scattering—Read the Tower of Babel story and Acts 2. Write a mission statement for your congregation.

3. Missions—Hear about the work of missionaries.

4. Music—Learn to sing "We Are the Church" with motions and teach it to the congregation.

5. Birthday Party—Decorate cake for the "birthday party."

6. Languages—Talk about the experience of speaking in tongues.

7. Waiting—Spend time in prayer and meditation.

8. Jesus Loves Me—Learn "Jesus Loves Me" in different languages.

9. Charades—Do exercises in universal understanding.

Gathering Again

Worship Drama

Hymn

Offering
(response of the activity groups)

Hymn . . . . "In Christ There Is No East or West"

Benediction

Birthday Party

The Celebration

Cover the front door of the church with bright birthday wrapping paper and ribbon. Add a bow and balloons to the church sign and a large "Happy Birthday, Church" card over the door if possible.

Gathering

Greeters welcome people to Pentecost, the church's birthday party, saying, "Good morning, happy birthday." Ushers hand out noisemakers (homemade or store bought) with the bulletin.

Inside, items symbolizing mission, such as a globe, the Bible, food, suitcases, and a foreign language phrase book, are arranged on the worship table.

Call to Worship

In the story of the Tower of Babel, the people were afraid of being separated. They said, "Come, let us make a name for ourselves; otherwise we shall be scattered abroad upon the face of the whole earth." But God wanted the people to be scattered and to carry the message far and wide, so God confused their language so that they could not communicate. They were forced to go away to find others who spoke their language. "The Lord scattered them abroad from there over the face of all the earth." At Pentecost people from every nation and every tongue came back together again. They could not speak one another's language, but they understood each other perfectly, because they were bound by a common faith. As we are gathered here today, let us remember that we are united to our brothers and sisters all over the world by faith, the universal language.

Hymn

"Pour Out Your Spirit" *or* "Let There Be an Anointing of the Spirit" *or* "O Holy Spirit Making Whole"

Reading

Leader:
(solemnly) In the beginning God formed Adam, first human, of the dust of the earth. And God breathed into first human the breath of life, and Adam, first human, became a living being.

(with animation) At the Pentecost, God rushed in as wind, filling people with the Holy Spirit, and the church became a living being to do God's work. This is the birthday of the church and its mission. Happy birthday to the church!

All:
(Make a racket with noisemakers.)

Leader:
Listen now. Be attentive to your breathing, breathing in and out, in and out *(pause)*. Breathing in, we pray, "Come Holy Spirit, enter" *(pause)*. Breathing out, we pray that God will drive out all that is unworthy *(pause)*. Thank God for the gift of the Spirit who fills us and gives us life.

Prayers

Silent Prayer

Congregational Prayer
The pastor or lay leader says:

Sensing with every breath that God is in our presence, offer your sentence prayers aloud if you feel called.

(Allow sentence prayers from the congregation.)

Hymn

"God of Grace and God of Glory"

Dance

"Spirit of the Living God"

One to three dancers can create dramatic movement to the hymn "Spirit of the Living God." Try making one dancer look like two by having him or her dance behind a curtain made of plain white sheets illuminated by two bright lamps. When the lamps are positioned 12-15 feet or 4-5 meters behind the curtain and 12-15 feet or 4-5 meters apart, they cast two shadows of one dancer to make it appear there are two dancers.

(First time) flute solo

(Second time) flute and dancers

(Third time) flute, dancers, and congregation singing

Scripture

A youth sits on a tall stool, writing at a desk or lectern, and begins to speak.

In the first book, Theophilus, I wrote about all that Jesus did and taught from the beginning until the day when he was taken up to heaven, after giving instructions through the Holy Spirit to the apostles whom he had chosen.

Youth looks up, sees that the congregation is listening, and talks excitedly to them.

Oh, my name is Luke. I was a follower of Jesus and now I am writing to my friend Theophilus to tell him all about the exciting day of Pentecost.

Pentecost means fiftieth. It comes from the fifty days after Passover. To the Jews it was a harvest festival. But we know it since that exciting day as the day God filled all the followers of Jesus with the Holy Spirit and gave us a mission. What a day that was! It started in an upper room where we, the followers of Jesus, had gathered. Before Jesus left us, he told us not to go anywhere or do anything. We were just supposed to wait for the power. And so we were waiting, and on Pentecost we got the power!

I want to tell my friend Theophilus every detail. It was some day! The birthday of the church!

Luke returns to his writing.

Activities

A leader says,

At Pentecost we celebrate the church and its mission, our congregation, churches in our denomination, churches around the world. We're all going to prepare now for our Pentecost celebration. Everybody is going to have a part.

The leader asks everyone to choose an activity and gives directions to activity centers.

Each person will have time for only one activity. They may choose so long as there is room in a group. When groups are full, encourage people to choose another. Some of the groups will be sharing with the congregation when they return.

1. Bible Study on Wind and Fire. Look up Bible stories about wind and fire, such as Genesis 8:1; Psalm 78:39; John 3:8; Exodus 3; 1 Kings 18, Matthew 3:11. What does "wind" or "fire" signify in each case? What are the properties of wind and fire that remind us of God? Do you see God at work in destructive winds or fire? Why or why not? What do wind and fire mean today? Ask a Bible study leader to prepare ahead of time by reading commentaries or a Bible dictionary. As a group, name one place in the world where the Spirit is at work. Be prepared to share this case in one sentence with the congregation.

2. Bible Study on Scattering. Compare the Tower of Babel story with Acts 2. Name other Bible stories about scattering for mission (Gen. 1:28; Gen. 11:1-9; Prov. 11:24 KJV; Mark 6:7-13; 16:15; Acts 2; 1 Pet. 1:1-2). What is your personal mission? What is your congregation's mission. Try writing a mission statement for the group. Then write a mission statement for yourself. If people are willing, share your personal statements. Does your church have a tendency to stick together like the people in Genesis? Why? What scares you about going out with the gospel? Be prepared to share your mission statement with the congregation.

3. Missions. Invite missionaries and volunteers from foreign missions and projects to talk about their decision to be mission workers. Also invite a person from a home mission. How are they different? How are they alike? What is your denomination's philosophy of mission? (Do you focus on conversion, church planting, service, education, or some other goal?) What steps could your congregation take to be more supportive of missionaries or be more mission-minded? Be ready to name three fears that keep many people from being mission workers.

4. Music. Form an intergenerational choir and dance troupe. Children especially will like this activity. Divide the group into pairs. Practice singing the song "We Are the Church" with movements by Avery and Marsh for the refrain (p. 59). Create new movements for each verse. Be prepared to lead the congregation in learning the song and motions. The Pentecost celebration will be enhanced if participants wear colorful costumes and hats and carry streamers on wands.

5. Birthday Party. Help decorate sheet cakes or cupcakes for the birthday party that will happen after worship. See how many happy birthday songs people in the group know. Be prepared to sing different versions.

6. Languages. Talk about the experience of speaking in tongues. What does that mean to people in the group? What is it like? Look at the Tower of Babel story in Genesis 11 and Pentecost in Acts 2, and discuss the following questions: Does language keep you from going places or visiting people? How would you rate your tolerance of other cultures and people who speak other languages? Have people who know a non-English language teach others to say "happy birthday" or "praise the Lord" in their language. Share the expressions at the birthday party.

7. Waiting. Jesus told the disciples to wait. Find a quiet place to spend time in prayer and meditation. Pray for the indwelling of the Spirit in your life and the courage to go out in mission.

8. Jesus Loves Me. Children and adults will enjoy learning "Jesus Loves Me" in one or more languages. Talk about how we cannot understand the foreign words, but that we know by the tune ex-

---

Worship Drama: Upper Room

(Jesus' followers are positioned motionless in the "Upper Room." The sound effects group is off to the side with a microphone.)

Narrator: Ten days after Jesus returned to heaven, the Israelites celebrated one of their important church festivals. It was called Pentecost or Feast of the Harvest. The purpose of the feast was to thank and praise God for all the harvest, which had been gathered and stored away.

Many people came to Jerusalem for the feast. Many of them were from foreign lands, and they spoke a variety of dialects and languages. Some were from the neighborhood of Persia, others from Egypt, still others from Arabia, faraway Rome, and other places. The streets of Jerusalem were crowded with people as they made their way to the temple to bring a thank offering and to praise God for his goodness.

(Pause—have several people who can speak non-English languages come out of the pews speaking as they come to the front, preferably in costume. They can be saying "Praise the Lord" in a variety of languages. They position themselves opposite the Upper Room sign.)

Early in the morning on the day of Pentecost, 120 followers of Jesus, including the apostles and Mary the mother of Jesus, were together in one place. They were

waiting for the Holy Spirit to come, whom Jesus had promised to send.

(Actors in the upper room come alive and pretend to be conversing, eating, working, or playing.)

About nine o'clock, while the disciples were praying, *(they kneel)* there was a strange noise. It sounded like a mighty blast of wind.

(Sound effects group says "shhh . . ." into a microphone or rub hands together gently at first and then harder near the microphone.)

It sounded like a mighty blast of wind!

(The off-stage fan, aimed at the upper room, is turned on.)

It came down from heaven and went to the room in which the disciples were gathered, filling it completely.

(Disciples jump up and look all around.)
(The fan goes off.)

The people in Jerusalem heard the noise, too. Greatly excited, they came running, *(a group runs up the center aisle showing excitement with hand gestures)* wondering what had happened.

actly what the song says because it is so familiar. Compare this to the believers' experience at Pentecost. Provide minimal costuming to represent different languages, such as a sombrero for Spanish, wooden shoes for German or Dutch, and a tunic for African languages. If there is time, also sing "Jesus Loves the Little Children." Perform "Jesus Loves Me" later in worship.

9. Charades. To encourage participants to think globally, do some of these exercises in universal understanding.

a. Play charades in which participants try to express themselves in pantomime.

b. Watch part of a foreign film. What is understandable without understanding the language?

c. Watch a video on racism. Check with your denominational headquarters or order from EcuFilm: "Bill Cosby on Prejudice," "The Boy King," "Eye of the Storm," "Our Father," "The Silver Stream," "The War Between the Classes." A 19-minute video titled "True Colors," taken from a segment of ABC's "Prime Time," is available for rental from Brethren Press (800 441-3712).

d. Compare a Mercator Projection Map (the kind found in most classrooms) with the Peters Projection Map (available from Friendship Press, P.O. Box 37844, Cincinnati, OH 45237). Discuss attitudes about race and nationality.

e. Invite an exchange student to talk about the experience of coming to a new culture.

f. Learn the song "Jesus, Pour Out Your Spirit" and create movements to go with it. Be prepared to share the song during worship.

Gathering Again

Use live or recorded flute music to suggest the presence of the Holy Spirit as people gather again in the sanctuary. The pastor or lay leader should instruct those people who have something to

---

(Lights go down. Disciples shine flashlights with orange and red filters made from plastic report covers to simulate flames.)

When they arrived at the place where the disciples were staying, they saw something that looked like a little flame of fire, shaped like a tongue, on the head of each of the disciples.

(They point at the disciples. The action freezes.)

(Lights come up.)

The Holy Spirit made the disciples brave and eager to go out and tell people about Jesus the Savior. The Spirit also made them able to speak languages they could not speak before.

(Disciples mingle with people from Jerusalem and the people who speak other languages. They are speaking "in tongues" excitedly.)

Now they could tell the people of various nations about Jesus the Savior, using their own languages.

The disciples lost no time in making use of the power they had just received. They stepped before the crowd around them and began speaking about the mighty deeds of God.

(The disciples depart in every direction, saying, in various languages if they are able, "God be praised!")

But the disciples weren't the only ones who heard and felt the wind and saw the tongues of fire. The Jews who had come to Pentecost did too. And they asked, "What does it mean?" Then Peter spoke.

Peter: *(Peter reads Acts 2:14b-21.)*

Narrator: And he told them how Jesus, who was crucified but rose from the dead, was the Lord and Messiah. And now, just as Jesus had promised, the Holy Spirit has been given. And when the people heard it, they were filled with fear and awe and they said, "What must we do?"

Peter: "Repent and be baptized."

Narrator: And they were! In one day 3,000 were baptized. They baptized day and night. It was amazing! But that wasn't the end either. The new believers devoted themselves to study and prayer and fellowship and baking bread. And they did many signs and wonders. And every day there were more believers. And that's how the church got started.

present to sit near the front and be prepared to give their response after the worship drama. Give each their lead-in line and speaking order.

Worship Drama

See "Upper Room," pages 56-57.

Hymn

"Move in Our Midst" or the Taizé hymn "Veni Sancte Spiritus" or any prayer hymn

Offering

Worship leader:

The story has been told. I wonder what it felt like to receive the Holy Spirit at Pentecost? I wonder what the people did after Pentecost? I wonder what we will do now that we've heard the story of Pentecost?

(The activity groups respond.)

Wind and fire group:

I know what we can do. We can wait on the Holy Spirit just as the disciples did. We have seen the Holy Spirit at work . . . *(name the instance).*

Scatter group:

We wrote a mission statement for our group. *(Read the statement.)*

Missions group:

We're afraid to go out with the good news because . . . *(name three fears),* but we're praying for courage.

Music and dance group:

We want to share the good news in song and dance. *(Participants sing "We Are the Church.")*

"Jesus Loves Me" group:

We're learning different languages so we can talk to people all over the world. *(Participants sing "Jesus Loves Me" in several languages.)*

Charades group:

We're disciplining ourselves to think globally. Though we don't speak the same language in the world, we are trying to communicate in the universal language of God's love. We want to sing and interpret a song about our dream for unity in God's world. *(The group sings and moves to "Jesus, Pour Out Your Spirit.")*

Hymn

"In Christ There Is No East or West" or other appropriate hymn from your congregation's hymnal (to lively banjo accompaniment)

Benediction

Once we waited in silence and fear
Once we were no people.
But God has made us a people.
The Holy Spirit has breathed on us.
We go forth filled, empowered.
As the living presence of Christ
   in the World
Praise be to God.

Birthday Party

End the celebration with a birthday party. Serve the decorated cakes.

Clypping

Clypping—meaning to surround closely, clasp, or embrace—is an old English tradition for Pentecost. The custom celebrates the love for the church. The entire congregation clasps hands and encircles the church building. While holding hands, sing happy birthday songs and walk or dance around the church. Be sure to use the noisemakers! For a variation, have children make red paper chains to encircle the church, or wrap the church in a big red bow. If weather forces you inside, form a ring around the sanctuary and sing.

We are the church

Text and Music: Richard Avery and Donald Marsh

Copyright © 1972 by Hope Publishing Co., Carol Stream, IL 60188. All rights reserved. Used by permission. This song may not be reproduced without permission of Hope Publishing Co.

Motions

Sing the song, and do the song—using gestures and movement with a different partner on each chorus. Enhance a Pentecost celebration with colorful costumes, hats, streamers on wands.

I am the church *(with thumb point to self)*
You are the church *(point to partner)*
All who follow Jesus *(reach out with both hands)*
All around the world *(encircle arms over head)*
Yes, we're the church together. *(link arms)*

Celebrating the Family
God's Plan for Relationships

A celebration of respect, love, and trust

> After a certain age, the more one becomes oneself, the more obvious one's family traits become.
>
> —*Marcel Proust*

Families are a place where people first become individuals. When our parents give us a name, it is the first step toward becoming a person in our own right. A name is unique, and many times it carries special meaning. When someone says a name, it brings to mind a person with a unique combination of traits and everyone knows who is being talked about. However, we are no one by ourselves. We get life from two others. We get personality and physical characteristics from family. And it is in the family where we acquire values and the art of relating. In a healthy family, we are not only loved, but we learn to love, respect, and trust others. In growing as individuals, we also become more intricately related to our families and the people around us, as well as to the whole interconnected world.

The church, of all places, needs to be a place where God's plan for the family is celebrated and proclaimed. God made family and planned that children would learn to know and love the Lord in the bosom of the family. We celebrate family, for it is God's beautiful place for naming, respecting, loving, trusting, relating, and growing in faith. As family members experience worth, belonging, and security in their home, they will come to know God as a loving parent and all people as brothers and sisters.

Bible Scope

Luke 15

Bible Text

Luke 15:11-32

**Bible Background
for Our Celebration**

In the story of the Prodigal Son, the father becomes a symbol for the forgiveness of God. He has a son who tests his patience, going against every rule. First the son asks for his inheritance while his father is still living. Then he asks for half the inheritance rather than the third that a younger son would normally receive. When the son willfully squanders the money and returns home, he has no reason to think his father would or should forgive him. But there is evidence the father's forgiveness began in his heart as he waited. "While he was still far off, his father saw him and was filled with compassion (Luke 15:20). Without knowing his son was repentant, he was ready to forgive him.

In that day and culture, a father would not have run to his son. This father, however, threw culture and caution to the wind and ran to meet the lost child. In an explosion of joy, the father hugged and kissed the son. But the father not only demonstrated unconditional love and forgiveness, he also showed great trust. He had to have been trusting in order to give the son his inheritance early. And he was respectful, regarding one son as much as the other though the children were very different. The story of the Prodigal Son is famous for its multiple and rich meanings, but it is especially significant for this celebration because it demonstrates the traits of a strong family—love, trust, and respect. Moreover, it is within the family that the young man learned the limits of his individuality and the value of healthy relationships. Strong Christian families and church families don't just happen. They are nurtured, formed, and built with great effort. And many times, we learn the hard way, just like the younger son. And like the biblical family, we seize every opportunity to celebrate our successes with joy and abandon.

Faith Nugget

A parent's love for a child is like God's love for us.

Early Preparation

A planning committee may want to consider holding the family celebration in May, which is Mother's Day month. Recently, it has been suggested that May be Christian family month in the church to recognize the importance of family in the Christian faith.

Gather symbols of the Christian family to decorate the worship center and create a visual reminder of family. For example, borrow a large dollhouse to represent family and home. Add a set of keys for trust, a telephone or note pad for good communication, a heart for love, a cross for Christ, and a collection of cassettes or albums from easy listening to rock to show respect for family members' individuality.

If possible, make the worship area look like a home. Put a rocking chair or an overstuffed chair and newspaper in the scene, or drape clothes over the worship table and scatter shoes, boots, mittens, and hats around. Perhaps a kitchen look is easier to represent. Load up a dish drainer with dishes and put it in the worship center.

The first part of the celebration will take place around tables in "family groups." As people arrive, each person will get a slip of colored paper. They should proceed to the table with a tablecloth of the same color. Young children may stay with parents, but everyone else should enter the mix. Ahead of time, collect enough mateless socks for everyone to have one. The socks symbolize the fact that everyone belongs, yet each is an individual—not to mention that every family mysteriously ends up with scads of mateless socks after laundry day! Cover tables with colorful tablecloths, and provide materials to assist in making nametags, including baby-naming books, genealogies, Bibles, and dictionaries.

You will need

- ☐ symbols of the Christian family
- ☐ family group leaders, activity leaders, storyteller, worship leader, readers
- ☐ household articles/furniture representing a home
- ☐ food for party scene
- ☐ colorful tablecloths

- ❏ leaders and supplies for activity centers
- ❏ a copy of *The Runaway Bunny* by Margaret Wise Brown
- ❏ slips of colored paper
- ❏ stick-on nametags, pins, and mateless socks
- ❏ baby-naming books, genealogies, Bible

Name of your church

Celebrating the Family
God's Plan for Relationships

Gathering

Processional . . . . "Sing Amen"

Call to Worship

Greetings

Litany

Readings

Children's Story. . . *The Runaway Bunny*

Hymn. . . . . "God Is So Good"

Prayers. . . . . Silent Prayer
and Pastoral Prayer

Scripture Dramatized . . . . Luke 15:11-32

Reading

Hymn of Response . . . . . . "Far, Far Away"

Activities

1. Communication Skills—Learn how to communicate better within the family.

2. Trusting and Respecting—Tips on how to build trust and respect among family members.

3. Names—Children get a chance to name themselves and others.

4. Singles—What does family mean for singles?

5. Sibling Rivalry—A look at the challenges that face brothers and sisters.

6. Inheritance—Adults discuss the problems of inheritance.

7. Turning the Tables—What happens when adults end up caring for elderly parents?

8. Masks—Children learn communication skills through making masks.

9. Roleplay—How is the story of the Prodigal Son different if studied from the older son's view, a daughter's perspective, or the wealthy parent's view?

Gathering Again

Offering

Hymn. . . . . . "Blest Be the Tie That Binds"

Benediction

The Celebration

A congregation is a family. At its best, the congregation loves, respects, and trusts its members, even the difficult ones. It provides a place where people grow and mature. It gives us a corporate identity and helps us find our individual identity. Today, in the comfort of the congregation, we are going to explore what it means to be family and how the church can help us be better families.

Gathering

As people arrive, have greeters meet them at the door with colored slips of paper. Everyone proceeds to the fellowship hall or classrooms to find their new family group by matching their colored slips of paper to colored tablecloths. Younger children may stay with a parent or go to their regular nursery room. Everyone else gets a new family for the first part of the day. Ahead of time, assign a host at each table who can lead the activity.

For an opening activity, everyone will talk about their names. What does my name mean? Who is my namesake? What if I had been born a boy instead of a girl? What would I like my name to be? This activity is designed to help people see they are both an individual with a unique name and part of a family who gave them a name and helped shape their identity.

Let people browse through dictionaries of names, baby-naming books, and genealogies, looking for the meaning of their names. Invite people to tell stories of how they got their names. Challenge people to trace their family lineage in a pattern of "begats." For example, "I am Lisa, daughter of Donna, daughter of Marilyn, daughter of Mary," and so on. If you have old church pictorial directories, let people try to identify out-of-date photos of people. Provide materials for making nametags. On a stick-on nametag, include your name and any other ways you are known, such as "son of John and Mary" or Social Security number or professional title or other distinguishing title. Adhere the nametag to one of the unique socks provided at the table, and pin the nametag and sock to your clothing.

The host wraps up the nametag activity saying something like:

In our service today we are going to celebrate the family. We are going to talk about the importance of family as the place we learn first-hand about God's plan for us to love, respect, trust, and communicate.

Processional

After this opening activity, reunite real families, including singles with adoptive families if they wish, and move to the sanctuary. As you process, sing "Sing Amen" (p. 69), repeating the first verse as often as needed. Or sing it antiphonally or in parts.

Call to Worship
The leader says:

You, O Lord, are in the midst of us, and we are called by your name; do not forsake us!
(Jer. 14:9b)

Greetings
Invite everyone to greet people around them, saying, "I am named
_____. What is your name?"

Litany

One:
Let us praise God for the simple joy of being together as family, whatever form of family we experience.

People:
Thanks be to God!

One:
For the joy of working together

People:
Thanks be to God!

One:
For the fun of playing together

People:
Thanks be to God!

One:
For the comfort of being gathered around the table with good food

People:
Thanks be to God!

One:
For the strength that comes from praying together

People:
Thanks be to God!

Readings

Youth reader says:

I have a name.

My parents gave me the beginning of a name.

They told the world, "Here is a person. He/she has a place among human beings."

People call me by name.

By this they say, "I want you to be present."

Sometimes it wonderfully means, "Hello there, freedom."

When a person calls to me by name, she is admitting me into the circle of people she recognizes as fellow humans. Into this cluster of people who believe in each other.

My name is shorthand for the fact that I mean something . . .

When people call me by name, I know that I am something distinctive.

Irreplaceable. Original poetry of the present. This particular vitality. A truth of falsehood that appears to them. A destiny.

O that I never become a number.

Or be anonymous in situations where I should be a name, and not be a blur.

—*Ross Snyder*
(Inscape)

Adult reader says:

When we respond to our names, or call someone else by name, it is already the beginning of a community expressing the image of God. To call someone by name is an act of prayer. We may abuse our names, and our prayer, but without names we are not human.

. . . . And we cannot name ourselves alone. Before we can love each other, before we can dialogue, each one of us has to be named by the other and we have to name in return.

—*Madeleine L'Engle*
(And It Was Good)

Children's Story

The suggested story, *The Runaway Bunny* by Margaret Wise Brown, is a well-known children's book and is available in most libraries and bookstores. To tell or read the story, gather the children around the storyteller who is sitting in a rocking chair or overstuffed chair, with a suitcase and a stuffed rabbit (or even a live one) at his or her feet.

To introduce the story, the storyteller says something like, "Have you ever felt like running away? Have you tried it? Do you have days when you just aren't getting along very well with people, maybe at school, or your family? Maybe you feel like you'd just like to trade in your whole family for another one! Or maybe you just feel like you'd like to sell your brother or sister the next time you have a garage sale but your mom says you can't. This story is called *The Runaway Bunny.*

Hymn

"God Is So Good" (p. 70)

Prayers

Silent Prayer

Pastoral Prayer

Dear God, you are Abba to us, a daddy. You are like the mother hen who gathers the chicks under her wing. You are the source of our being, our teacher, and the object of our childlike devotion. But we have not always been model children, we are not always trustworthy or respectful or honest. Yet you love us anyway and provide a home where we can learn to love, trust, and respect, a home called the church. And each time we come home to the church you welcome us with an embrace in spite of our failings in the preceding week. How good it is to be home in your loving care. Amen.

Dramatic Presentation of Luke 15:11-32

See page 66.

Reading

Adult woman reader says:

There is always something left to love. And if you ain't learned that, you ain't learned nothin' .... Child, when do you think is the time to love somebody the most; when they done good and made things easy for everybody? Well, then, you ain't through learning—because that ain't the time at all. It's when he's at his lowest and can't believe in hisself 'cause the world done whipped him so. When you starts measuring somebody, measure him right, child, measure him right. Make sure you

done taken into account what hills and valleys he come through before he got to whever he is.

—Lorraine Hansberry
(A Raisin in the Sun)

Hymn of Response

"Far, Far Away"

Activities

Give brief instructions for going to activity centers. The bulletin will contain the list and meeting places.

1. Communication Skills. Talk about difficulties you've experienced communicating in the family. Using actual or made-up cases, practice clear communication with active listening and "I" statements. Active listening is the skill of interpreting what someone is saying. It involves careful listening, distilling, and summarizing someone else's arguments and repeating them back to be sure you understand. For instance, you might say,

---

Dramatic Presentation of Luke 15:11-32

The parable family in biblical or contemporary costumes comes together at a table. In addition to the father, older son, and younger son, consider including a mother, additional younger children, and servants. Feature the three main characters at the table. The others are in the background. As the narrator and actors read the scriptures, the actors pantomime the scenes.

Narrator: Luke 15:11-12

The family is eating or busying themselves around the table. The father and younger son pantomime discussion.

Narrator: Luke 15:13a

The younger son leaves, going out through the sanctuary without looking back. The parents wave goodbye and the older brother sulks. All leave the stage.

Narrator: Luke 15:13b-16

At verse 14, the younger son appears from the rear of the sanctuary, looking disheveled, staggering to the front. At verse 16, he lies down as if bedding down with the hogs.

Narrator: Luke 15:17a

Younger Son: Luke 15:17b-19

The younger son pretends to walk, turning his body to the side while talking to the congregation.

Narrator: Luke 15:20

The younger son faces the center of the sanctuary, and the father and servants appear distantly in his view. When they finally see each other, father and son run to embrace.

Younger Son: Luke 15:21b *(to the father)*

Father: Luke 15:22b-24 *(to the servants)*

There is a flurry of activity. Servants, children, and the mother carry in trays of real food. Food might be a large sheet cake cut in small pieces, pretzels, loaves of bread. Children make celebrative sound with noisemakers. If you have a juggler or clowns in your congregation, include them in the party. Children take trays of food out into the congregation, passing food down the rows.

Narrator: Luke 15:25-28

When people have had a chance to eat, the actors freeze in place; the older brother appears on the other side of the sanctuary from the action, standing all alone; and the narrator reads verses 25-28. At verse 28, the father approaches the older son.

Older Son: Luke 15:29b-30

Father: Luke 15:31b-32

Everyone leaves the stage. Let silence fall over the congregation.

"It sounds to me like you don't want to go to school because the gym teacher always mentions your weight problem." Keep working at the same idea until you both agree on the interpretation.

"I" statements are sentences that tell exactly how you feel without being accusing. Instead of saying, "You always treat me like a little kid," you can say, "When you call me 'baby,' I feel like a child. I want you to treat me like a grownup."

Try roleplays that use active listening. Or make lists of arguments that are common in families and turn them into "I" statements, for example: "You're always driving the car but you never buy any gas"/"I really feel inconvenienced when I always have to fill the car up with gas."

2. Trusting and Respecting. Begin by looking at the stories of Abraham and Ruth as examples of trust and respect. When did Abraham and Ruth show trust? respect? What problems with trust and respect do you have in your family? How can your family be more like those of Abraham and Ruth?

For fun, and to test your level of trust, have a trust walk. Set up several obstacles in the room. Blindfold one person at a time. Turn them several times to disorient them, and then guide them only with verbal commands through the obstacle course. Ask, "How much did you trust? Were you surprised by your feelings? What would make you more trustful?"

Trust and respect result from being loved and valued. Trust especially comes from having these things consistently. Make a list of reasons why there is mistrust in your family and compare with other people in the group. Then focus on what it is you love about your family. Brainstorm ways to show appreciation, such as listening, complimenting, and encouraging family members. On small cards, write one compliment or encouraging thought for each member of your family, and slip them inside a school lunch bag, a briefcase, under a pillow, or in a coat pocket this week.

3. Names. Adults assist younger children (grades kindergarten through sixth grade) in giving new names to themselves, their friends, and their families. Help them draw a family tree with all new names for immediate family members, putting given names in parentheses. Using the dictionary of names, help them learn what their new name means. When each is finished, sit in a circle and share the new names. Have stick-on nametags available for each child's new name.

4. Singles. Although adolescents are looking for independence, many young adults are looking for attachments, relationship, and intimacy. Whether or not one plans to be married someday, there is a great deal of intimacy, a deep connectedness, in friendships and family. Intimacy doesn't have to be defined sexually or romantically. In fact, some of the most gratifying relationships are not romantic at all. Use this time to share with each other some of the problems of being single and some of the joys of the single life. As a group, come up with a definition of family for single people. Also talk about where you find family. How important is family to you, your own or a family you choose? For biblical examples, look at the stories of Jeremiah, Paul, Miriam, and Lydia.

5. Sibling Rivalry. Whatever happens to families in our society seems to happen to families of the Bible as well. Cain and Abel, Jacob and Esau, and the older and younger brothers in Luke 15 all experienced sibling rivalry. So do we. Have participants tell stories of their experiences of sibling rivalry, either as a parent of sibling rivals or as a sibling rival themselves. Also have the parents talk about how they deal with favoritism. Are children right—does mom really love one more than another? Invite a family counselor to join the discussion and suggest ways to deal with rivalry and favoritism.

6. Inheritance. Have you faced the problems that the loving father faced regarding inheritance in the parable of the Prodigal Son? How can you divide up your wealth and possessions fairly among your children and charities? Should you do it while you're alive? Share your experiences and brainstorm with others about ways to distribute an inheritance. What will you leave your heirs besides money? Invite an administrator from a retirement home to talk about new ways to handle inheritance.

7. Turning the Tables. Very often the family roles of parent and child get switched when parents become elderly. Children become primary caretakers for older adults who can no longer take care of themselves. Study John 21:18 for biblical guidance. Compare stories with other families experiencing the same thing. Think of ways to support adult children and dependent parents in the difficult decisions and hard work they face. For instance, plan to organize "sitters" to relieve caretakers for several hours each week. Or arrange for drivers to take older parents to appointments and shopping. Write notes of encouragement to adult children and their dependent parents.

8. Masks. Help children learn how to express themselves clearly in their families by making masks for various emotions. Ask children to name as many feelings as they can. Then let them draw faces expressing those emotions on paper plates. Glue masks of opposite feelings back to back with a tongue depressor inserted between them for a handle. Have children practice expressing sadness, happiness, fear, anger, and other emotions.

9. Roleplay. The story of the Prodigal Son might sound different if we could hear the older brother's version. What would the story be like if a daughter squandered her inheritance or if she stayed behind to be the "good child"? Or how would the story be told from a mother's point of view? Role play several versions of the story using a different point of view each time or featuring different characters. Ask, "Which version means the most to you? Does the ending change, or does the parent always welcome the child? Does the child always want to come home?" Ask a clever writer in the group to script several versions and act them out for Sunday school classes in the coming weeks.

Gathering Again

Everyone gathers in the sanctuary or fellowship hall for a closing.

Offering

Hymn

"Blest Be the Tie That Binds"

Benediction

Father of orphans and protector of widows is God in his holy habitation. God gives the desolate a home to live in.

(Ps. 68:5-6b)

Now may God, the parent of all families, the one who sets all of us in families, bless you, sustain you, strengthen you in God's love to be a family to those who need your love. Amen.

For an alternative benediction that would appeal to children, play "Bear Hug" from the cassette *All God's Creatures Are Special* by Jingle Jam. You might also consider sending families away with a single candle, suggesting that they set aside a special time each week to light the candle and gather as a family for five minutes in gratitude for the gift of family.

Sing amen

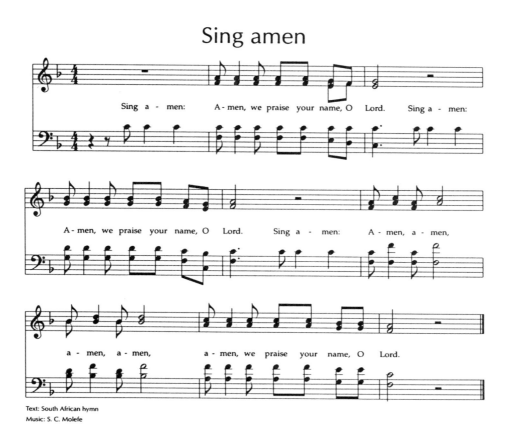

Text: South African hymn
Music: S. C. Molefe

God is so good

God is so good,
God is so good,
God is so good,
God's so good to me.

God has named me,
God has named me,
God has named me.
God's so good to me.

Text: Traditional
Music: Traditional African

Celebrating Peace
God's Ambassadors of Reconciliation

A celebration of our ability to be peacemakers

7

> Never doubt that a small group of thoughtful, committed citizens can change the world; indeed, it's the only thing that ever has.
>
> *—Margaret Mead*

> Everybody can be great. Because anybody can serve. You don't have to have a college degree to serve. You don't have to make your subject and your verb agree to serve ... You only need a heart full of grace. A soul generated by love.
>
> *—Martin Luther King, Jr.*

Robert Frost said, "The Sermon on the Mount is just a frame-up to insure the failure of all of us ...." Though skeptics such as Frost believe that the Sermon on the Mount is merely an ideal we can never achieve, it is perhaps the most practical passage in all the Bible. It is at least as practical as returning evil for evil. Gandhi pointed out that resorting to an eye for an eye and a tooth for a tooth only succeeds in making everyone blind and toothless. Not a very practical notion.

As a practical matter, peace is something all of us can pursue and is required of us as Christians. As Margaret Mead and Martin Luther King say, service is not reserved for the educated and the eloquent. The common people working together make the greatest difference in the world. This event is to celebrate the contributions of ordinary people to peace and justice. And though we are not near achieving world peace, we celebrate as an act of hope in the possibility of life and peace for the future. "Let us then pursue what makes for peace and for mutual upbuilding" (Rom. 14:19).

Bible Scope
Matthew 5—7

Bible Text
Matthew 5—7

Bible Background for Our Celebration

Peace, or *shalom*, is a central theme in the New Testament account of Jesus' ministry. Broadly, shalom refers to God's will and vision for a harmonious world. More specifically, shalom encompasses well-being, wholeness, right relationships, and joyful celebration of life in addition to the absence of violence and oppression. From Jesus' birth and the angel's declaration of peace (Luke 2:14), to his first sermon introducing a plan of shalom for the poor, the brokenhearted, the prisoners, the blind, and the wounded (Luke 4:18-19), to his voluntary suffer-

ing on the cross, Jesus had a peace mission.

According to Galatians 5, Christians in the first century learned that anyone who followed Christ would produce fruits of the Spirit, namely love, joy, and peace, patience, kindness, generosity, faithfulness, gentleness, and self-control. God's vision is for Christians to continue the work Jesus began by taking on the mission of peace and bringing shalom to others (2 Cor. 5:18).

The biblical notion of peace is not only the peace of mind and spirit that comes with death and the rewards of the after-life. It is a peace for the present. The Sermon on the Mount is the Christian's practical peace guide for living a life of shalom here and now. For starters, it tells how to treat enemies, how to handle marital infidelity, how to avoid adultery, what to do about oaths, how to resist revenge, and how to pray. In general, it promotes a way of living, an attitude and an approach to life.

These teachings, Jesus said, do not replace the laws of the prophets; they fulfill the law. Shalom and the mission for peace were created at the beginning of the world, demonstrated by Adam and Eve, the garden of Eden, and Noah. Jesus uses the Sermon on the Mount to bring us back to God's original plan for unity and peace. Often, Christians mistakenly believe that Jesus rejected the Hebrew laws altogether in favor of a doctrine of grace. But in truth, Jesus gave us the fullest view of the law, a law that includes shalom and peace.

Faith Nugget
Fulfilling God's will for peace in the world is the job of every Christian.

Early Preparation

Many denominations have a peace Sunday or a peace week. Consider holding this celebration in conjunction with denominational programs or a patriotic holiday. Plan to hold the event outdoors in a park or on the church grounds with an alternate site in case of rain. This is a good opportunity to invite friends and neighbors who don't attend your church.

Acknowledging that cars contribute heavily to the destruction of environmental peace, encourage people to walk, carpool, use public transportation, ride horses, bikes, or in-line skates to the gathering place.

Flags are often a symbol of allegiance. Appoint someone to create a peace flag that symbolizes the Christian's allegiance to peace and unity. Use it to welcome people on the day of the celebration.

During the celebration, children will be invited to place a "peace toy" at the worship center. At least two weeks before the celebration, alert parents by letter and the church newsletter to bring toys that are peaceful, such as a stuffed globe, books, games, puzzles, kaleidoscopes, blocks, puppets, kites, and bubble solution.

Also, as part of the celebration, the congregation will dedicate a symbol of peace. Decide as a committee whether to hang a painting about peace, erect a statue of Saint Francis or other peace figure, or plant a peace pole. The 8-foot or 2.5 meter peace pole, like the one pictured at the beginning of this chapter, says "May peace prevail on earth" on each side in different languages of your choice and may be ordered from Peace Pole Makers USA, 3534 Lanham Road, Maple City, MI 49664, 616 334-4467.

You will need

- ❑ peace toys
- ❑ a wagon, sandbox, or child's wading pool
- ❑ a peace flag
- ❑ children's story about peace
- ❑ a peace pole or work of art for dedication
- ❑ people to research stories of peace heroes and heroines
- ❑ a host for the gathering activity
- ❑ leaders and material for activity centers
- ❑ readers

Name of your church

Celebrating Peace

God's Ambassadors of Reconciliation

Gathering

Passing the Peace

Peace Monument Dedication

Witness to Peace . . . . "What Can a Christian Do?"

Hymn. . . . "Let There Be Peace on Earth"

Prayer of Dedication

Dialog on Peacemaking

Anthem . . . . "Song of Hope"

Inspiration Through Story

Prayers

Children's Story

Hymn. . . . . "Dona Nobis Pacem"

Activities

1. Peace Toys—A look at toys and how they teach or don't teach peace to children.

2. Mediation—Children and adults learn the basics of mediation for solving conflicts productively and peacefully.

3. Peace Between Faiths—A Jew, a Muslim, and a Christian talk about their faith's desire for peace and promote understanding between religious groups.

4. Denominational Peace Witness—Learn what your denomination is doing for peace and how you can get involved.

5. Youth for Peace—Youth, who are approaching an age of decision, practice formulating a peace stance.

6. Vote for Peace—Write letters on peace issues to the president or prime minister and your representatives in Congress or Parliament.

7. Peace Games—Play noncompetitive games that require working together for fun.

8. Peace Pals—To promote understanding between peoples, correspond with people in a country where the church has a mission or service.

9. Peace Flags—Flags are a symbol of dedication. Make a flag or windsock that signifies your dedication to peace.

Gathering Again

Hymn. . . . . . . "You Are Salt for the Earth"

Offering

Reading

Benediction

Sending Forth

The Celebration

If you are erecting a peace pole, begin worship outside around the pole. If you are dedicating an object that can be displayed in the sanctuary, meet there.

Gathering

As people gather, have children take their peace toys to the worship center, placing them in or around the wagon, pool, or sandbox.

Passing the Peace

Open by passing the peace. Greet someone near you, saying, "The peace of God be with you." The person will respond by saying "And with you" and then turn to greet the next person until all have been greeted.

Peace Monument Dedication

Witness to Peace: "What Can a Christian Do?"

Ask someone in your congregation to give testimony to the centrality of peace in the gospel and the importance of everyone working for peace. Emphasize the power of even one person to make peace. Or tell "One Man's Story" on page 74.

Hymn

"Let There Be Peace on Earth"

If you are erecting a peace pole, consider having children weave streamers around the pole during the singing of "Let There Be Peace on Earth," such as would be performed with ribbons around a may pole.

Attach 6-8 crepe paper streamers (6 feet or 2 meters long) to the top of the peace pole. Have four children take hands and form a circle around the pole. Tell the children to drop hands and make a one quarter turn to their right so

---

One Man's Story

He came into the Sunday school room with a slight limp. Otherwise, there was nothing to prepare the group for the story he would tell.

The leader had just tried to show that the Bible pushes us toward a peace position, and he wondered if he had succeeded, when the man with the limp began to speak.

He said he grew up in a small community in that region. During his teenage years tensions heightened in Europe as war loomed and then burst upon the continent. By then, of course, his own country had become involved.

A draft was instituted to secure young men for the fight. He was under age—only 17 at the time—but felt the call to duty when the man down the street, a man with a wife and two children, received his notice to report. "I wanted to go in his place, being that he had a family," the man said. "I was patriotic and I was proud to go and defend my country. So I lied about my age and volunteered to take this man's place. Going to war got me this limp. It also got me memories that'll never leave me."

He went on: "After going through training, I ended up on the battlefield in Europe. I can still remember one particular day. We were locked in a pitched battle with the Germans, and were giving it all we had. I saw one of the enemy soldiers standing to fire. I got him in the sights of my rifle. I pulled the trigger. He fell."

There was a moment of silence. Then he began again: "I've been haunted by this ever since. Was it my bullet or somebody else's that killed him? I guess I'll never know."

There is a connection between human beings that even the passions of war cannot completely sever. God has placed within us a deep bond with other people, even though they may be on the other side of some dividing line, placed there by governments or racial groups or social class. Try as we might, and despite the best efforts of those who tell us to despise or kill others for some supposedly noble goal, this bond endures.

—Source unknown

they are looking at the back of the person formerly their right.

Have four other children take hands and form a larger outer circle around the first four children. Dropping hands, each child in this circle turns one quarter turn to the left so he or she is looking at the back of the person formerly on their left. Practice first without streamers. Ask each child to look to their right and slightly ahead at the approaching person in the opposite circle. These couples reach out and shake right hands. Then gently pull that person by and shake left hands with the child coming toward him or her. Those two pull by and reach out with right hands again, and so on around the circle.

Now give each child a streamer to hold. In the dance, children will not shake hands, but will pass right shoulders first, then left shoulders, in the same fashion as before, weaving in and out. Like a grand allemande in square dancing, the two circles will begin weaving in and out while moving in opposite directions. As they weave, children will hold the streamers at shoulder level, lifting them higher to pass over another child or dropping them lower to pass beneath another streamer. As they dance, the streamers will be woven over the pole.

Prayer of Dedication

Pastor or lay person says:

Prince of Peace, we dedicate this memorial today to remind us to

"Let love be genuine; hate what is evil, hold fast to what is good; love one another with mutual affection; outdo one another in showing honor."

We pray that it will encourage us to

"[Never] lag in zeal, be ardent in spirit, serve the Lord. Rejoice in hope, be patient in suffering, persevere in prayer. Contribute to the needs of the saints; extend hospitality to strangers."

May this monument instruct us to

"Bless those who persecute you; bless and do not curse them. Rejoice with those who

**rejoice, weep with those who weep. Live in harmony with one another; do not be haughty, but associate with the lowly; do not claim to be wiser than you are. Do not repay anyone evil for evil, but take thought for what is noble in the sight of all. If it is possible, so far as it depends on you, live peaceably with all."
Amen.**

—*adapted from Romans 12:9-18*

If you have been outdoors, move inside, singing "Amen" *or* "Peace Is Flowing Like a River."

Dialog on Peacemaking

See pages 76-77.

Anthem

"Song of Hope" (p. 81)

Inspiration Through Story

Ahead of time, assign up to ten people to tell the stories of peacemakers. For a more dramatic presentation, tell the stories in the first person. Actors may choose from the list of peacemakers below or suggest their own. Before the celebration, they should read something about the person and prepare 100-200 words telling one thing this person did for peace. Actors should scatter themselves in the congregation during the celebration. When it is time for their presentation, they may stand where they are and project their lines loudly and clearly. Portable microphones will help if you have them. If sound is a problem, consider having actors say their lines from the front, from a lectern, or from a microphone off stage.

Inspiring peacemakers: Samantha Smith, Anne Frank, Shel Silverstein, Sadako (*Sadako and the Thousand Paper Cranes*), Jesus, Thomas Merton, A. J. Muste, Dorothy Day, Mahatma Gandhi, Martin Luther King, Jr., Mother Teresa, Jane Addams, Bishop Desmond Tutu, Benjamin Linder, Harriet Tubman, Andre Trochme, Tich Naht Han, your denominational peacemakers.

Prayers

Pastor or lay leader asks the congregation to name aloud members who need prayers. He or she should also ask for prayers for peace for people the world over. Allow a period of silence to reflect on all the requests. End by leading the congregation in the World Peace Prayer.

**Lead me from death to life
From falsehood to truth
Lead me from despair to hope
From fear to trust
Lead me from hate to love
From war to peace
Let peace fill our hearts, our world,
    our universe**

—Project Ploughshares

Children's Story

Choose from such stories as *White Feather* by Ruth Eitzen, *Potatoes Potatoes* by Anita Lobel, *The Story of Ferdinand* by Munro Leaf, *The Butter Battle Book* by Dr. Seuss, *The Weight of a Snowflake* (an East German folktale), or any children's story of peace from your local library.

Hymn

"Dona Nobis Pacem" can be sung in parts or as a round.

Activities

Instruct the congregation to choose an activity and proceed to a preassigned meeting space.

1. Peace Toys. The Peace Resource Center of San Diego (5717 Lindo Paseo, San

Dialogue on Peacemaking

In this dialog Readers 1 & 2 recite some of their lines at the same time. Where marked, Reader 2 begins speaking simultaneously with Reader 1.

Reader 1:
But I say to you that listen, Love your enemies, *(Reader 2 begins to read simultaneously)* do good to those who hate you, bless those who curse you, pray for those who abuse you. If anyone strikes you on the cheek, offer the other also; and from anyone who takes away your coat do not withhold even your shirt.

Reader 2:
Iraq, Iran, Germany, Japan, Serbia, Croatia, northern and southern Sudan; Muslims and Christians in Nigeria, Protestants and Catholics in Northern Ireland, Hindus and Sikhs in India . . .

Reader 1:
Hey, cut it out! I'm trying to tell people about loving their enemies.

Reader 2:
Yeah? Well, I'm just telling you that in real life it's pretty hard for people to settle their conflicts without violence!

Reader 1:
You have heard that it was said, "You should love your neighbor and hate your enemy." *(Reader 2 begins to read simultaneously)* But I say to you, love your enemies and pray for those who persecute you, so that you may be children of your Father in heaven; for he makes his sun to rise on the evil and on the good and sends rain on the righteous and on the unrighteous.

Reader 2:
China occupying Tibet, Israel occupying the West Bank; the military occupying Haiti; the lands of native peoples occupied everywhere by everybody. Guatemala and Burma killing their own people, nuclear weapons and not-so-smart smart bombs ready to kill anybody's people.

Diego, CA 92115) publishes a pamphlet called "Values Through Toys." Present the information in the pamphlet and talk with parents about the effect of certain toys on the behavior and values of young children. Make a list of toys that promote peaceful values and good fun. Distribute the list to others in the church near Christmas.

2. Mediation. Invite a conflict mediator to train church people in the basics of mediation for solving conflicts productively and peacefully. Peace groups, schools, social workers, pastors, and organizations for legal alternatives often have trained conflict mediators on their staffs. If a trainer is not available, you may wish to order information:

Community Boards
149 Ninth Street
San Francisco, CA 94103
415 552-1250

George Mason University
Center for Conflict Resolution
4400 University Drive
Fairfax, VA 22030
703 323-2038

**Children's Creative
Response to Conflict**
P.O. Box 271
Nyack, NY 10960
914 358-4601

**Martin Luther King, Jr.,
Center for Social Change**
449 Auburn Avenue, NE
Atlanta, GA 30312
404 524-1956

3. Peace Between Faiths. Invite a Jew, a Muslim, and a Christian to talk about his or her faith's desire for peace and understanding between religious groups. If you live in a rural area without repre-

---

Reader 1:
Listen, this is a church service. There's a time and a place for what you're saying; but not here, not now!

Reader 2:
There's no better place than the house of God to talk about the pain of the people of God because of the violence of war and racism and poverty.

Reader 1:
If you love those who love you, what credit is that to you? *(Reader 2 begins to read simultaneously)* For even sinners love those who love them. If you do good to those who do good to you, what credit is that to you? For even sinners do the same. But love your enemies, do good, and lend, expecting nothing in return. Your reward will be great, and you will be children of the Most High, who is kind to the ungrateful and the wicked.

Reader 2:
Los Angeles, New York, and everywhere in between; black and white, red and brown, rich and poor, insiders and outsiders. Skinheads, KKK, Black Panthers, White Nation; pro-choice, pro-life; liberals and evangelicals. Men abusing women, parents hurting children. So many people hurting from so many things.

Reader 1:
All right, I've finished. What if they missed all that I was saying and only heard what you were saying?

Reader 2:
But what if they had heard only what you were saying without hearing what I had to say?

—David Radcliff

If you live in a rural area without representatives from other faiths, invite people of different denominations, cultures, races, or ages to talk about understanding another's way of life. Consider questions such as:

What is the divine will for peace in your tradition?

How are our traditions alike when it comes to peace? How are they different?

Who are the peace heroes from your tradition?

What are the people from your tradition doing for peace?

How can we work together?

4. Denominational Peace Witness. Talk with a staff person at your denomination's headquarters about what the church is doing for peace. Order denominational peace literature. Invite a denominational peacemaker to tell the group what your denomination is doing for peace and suggest ways you can get involved. With a leader or on your own, talk about how you personally are affected by war (as a taxpayer, employee, parent, voter), how you can or cannot affect peace, how you can make peace in the community, how you can make peace in the nation or world.

5. Youth for Peace. Youth are approaching an age of decision, an age in which they will be asked to express their beliefs about peace at the military recruiting office, in the voting booth, and in the church board room. Help them formulate their own individual peace stance. Some denominational headquarters will keep statements by youth on file to demonstrate their earnest commitment to peace. Such statements can be used in building a defense for Selective Service. For information contact National Interreligious Service Board for Conscientious Objectors (NISBCO) or Central Committee for Conscientious Objectors (CCCO):

NISBCO
1601 Connecticut Avenue, N.W.
Washington, DC 20009-1035
202 482-4510

CCCO
2208 South Street
Philadelphia, PA 19146
215 545-4628

6. Vote for Peace. Set up a writing station where children, youth, and adults can make themselves heard by writing letters on peace issues to the president or prime minister and representatives in Congress or Parliament. Provide paper, pens, envelopes, stamps, addresses. Also bring recent news magazines for handy reference on the issues.

The President

The President
The White House
Washington, DC 20500

Dear Mr. President:

Very respectfully yours,

Prime Minister

The Prime Minister
House of Commons
Ottawa, ON K1A 0K2

Dear Mr. Prime Minister:

Very respectfully yours,

U.S. Senators

The Honorable [full name]
United States Senate
Washington, DC 20510

Dear Senator [last name]:

Sincerely yours,

Canadian Senators

The Honorable [full name]
Canadian Senate
Ottawa, ON K1A 0K2

Dear Senator [last name]:

Sincerely yours,

U.S. Representatives

The Honorable [full name]
House of
    Representatives
Washington, DC 20515

Dear Mr./ Ms. [last name]

Sincerely yours,

Member of Parliament

The Honorable [full name]
House of Commons
Ottawa, ON K1A 0K2

Dear Mr. / Ms. [last name]

Sincerely yours,

7. Peace Games. Check out a book of noncompetitive games from your local library. Explain to the participants that these are more than games. They help us learn how to get along and to actually help each other instead of trying to defeat each other. Emphasize that Jesus taught us in the Sermon on the Mount to reject revenge and to help everybody win. Play as many games as time allows. Consider reflecting after each game on how it feels to cooperate. Do some people feel more involved than they usually do in games? Compare feelings after these games to the feelings produced by win/lose games.

8. Peace Pals. To promote understanding between the world's future leaders, have children correspond with children in a country where the church has a mission or service project. Contact your denominational offices for suggestions. Provide paper, pencils and pens, crayons, envelopes, stamps, and addresses. Encourage children to write about or draw pictures of life in their country. Suggest to children that they share favorite songs, games, and stories. Tell about a typical day in their life, or talk about what they would like to do when they are adults. Their letters may lead to continued correspondence and friendships.

9. Peace Flags. National flags are a symbol of allegiance. Make a flag or windsock that signifies the group's allegiance to peace, or let each person make a small flag to take home. Use a sturdy fabric such as nylon or heavy cotton. Glue on or applique peace symbols (e.g., dove, olive branch, handshake, globe, cross) made from the same material as the flag, and hang it in the church or at home.

Gathering Again

Hymn

"You Are Salt for the Earth" by Marty Haugen

The Bible in Pieces

A young man tells the story of how he discovered what the Bible says about peace and justice. At the time, he was working for the poor and attending a very affluent church. The congregation considered itself to be very biblically oriented, but on the question of peace and justice, they had very little to say. Sure, they conceded, the Bible teaches us to love each other, but it does not tell Christians to demonstrate, march, protest, and take nonviolent action.

This man said to himself, "If this church is made up of Bible-believing Christians and they don't find anything in the Bible that supports my work, maybe the Bible doesn't have anything to say about questions of social justice or the poor or economics. Maybe I need to either give up my work with the poor and immerse myself more in this church or leave the church and throw myself in with the poor without the support of my faith.

The disparity drove the man to a crisis of faith. Just what does the Bible teach? So he began to study the Bible himself. He scoured the scriptures, underlining every passage dealing with social justice or economics or the poor. When he set out, he wasn't sure he would find anything, but as he worked, he found he was doing an enormous amount of underlining. The gospel of peace and God's concern for the poor were everywhere in the Bible.

Then he took the scissors to the Bible and began to cut out the passages on peace and justice. He snipped and carved and cut until he had removed everything the Bible says about peace and justice and the poor. When he was done he held up a shredded book. The Bible without the message of social justice and God's concern for the poor and oppressed does not hold together.

Be peacemakers with the full force of the gospel in your hand and "Always be ready to make your defense to anyone who demands from you an accounting for the hope that is in you . . ." (1 Pet. 3:15).

Offering

Reading

Read "The Bible in Pieces" on page 79.

Benediction

Group 1: I am only one,

Group 2: But still I am one.

Group 1: I cannot do everything,

Group 2: But still I can do something;

All: And because I cannot do
everything
I will not refuse to do the
something
that I can do.

—Edward Everett Hale

Sending Forth

Sing "Go Now in Peace" *or* "You Shall
Go Out with Joy."

Song of hope

Text and Music: Jim Strathdee
Copyright © 1985 by Desert Flower Music, Carmichael, CA 95609

Celebrating Sabbath
Renewal of Body, Mind, and Spirit

A festival for God's redeeming grace

8

On the seventh day of creation, God created rest. Anna, the enigmatic little theologian in the classic, *Mister God, This Is Anna*, said,

"Why did Mister God rest on the seventh day?"

"I suppose he was a bit flaked out after six days' hard work," I answered.

"He didn't rest because he was tired, though."

"Oh, didn't he? It makes me tired just to think about it all."

"Course he didn't. He wasn't tired."

"Wasn't he?"

"No, he made rest."

"Oh. He did that, did he?"

"Yes, that's the biggest miracle. Rest is. What do you think it was like before Mister God started on the first day?"

"A perishing big muddle, I guess." I replied.

"Yes, and you can't rest when everything is in a big muddle."

—Fynn

How easy it is to let our minds get into a "perishing big muddle." God said, *remember* the sabbath (a job for the mind) and *keep* it (a job for the heart). Sabbath. Hold the word in your heart. Sabbath is a place in the heart, a place where body, mind, and spirit unite at the gentle candlelight invitation, "Come to the sabbath time." Sabbath is a call to remember, to remember God in rest and worship. Slow down and celebrate God's work and your work, the simple joys of kindling the sabbath candles, enjoying good food and the presence of family, friends, and neighbors.

Bible Scope
Genesis 2:2-3; Exodus 20:8-11; 1 Samuel 21:1-6; Mark 2:27

Bible Text
Exodus 20:8-11

Bible Background for Our Festival
Remembering the sabbath is the only one of the Ten Commandments that calls for festivity. For both Jewish and Christian traditions, it is the most frequently celebrated festival because it is observed every week. As God commands it in Exodus 20:8, we are to recall the pattern and rhythm of creation, in which the world was formed in six days and on the seventh day, God created a day

of rest and remembrance. We are to keep the sabbath holy by making it different from the other days of the week. By working six days we honor the dignity of work. By resting on the sabbath, we honor the holiness of God and the dignity and worth of people. We do this through good fellowship, worship, and contemplation. Over time, Jewish tradition developed very specific rules about how the sabbath should be celebrated, including what kind of activity could or could not take place on that day. Jesus objected to the rigidity of such sabbath practices, claiming that the sabbath was given to us for our need to rest. We were not made in order to carry out the rules slavishly. In fact, one important interpretation of the sabbath comes from Deuteronomy 5:12-15, another account of the Ten Commandments. Here Moses adds that God delivered us from slavery and after six days of work each week we should use the sabbath to remember God's justice and how we are redeemed.

Faith Nugget

"More than Israel has kept the sabbath, the sabbath has kept Israel."

—*Achad Haam, Jewish essayist*

Early Preparation

This celebration plan is modeled on the traditional observance of *shabbat* or sabbath, using elements of both Christian and Jewish practice since both claim the sabbath as heritage. As a family ritual kept primarily in the home, it is ideal for intergenerational festivities. Everyone will enjoy turning the church into one large home and family to observe the sabbath either on Sunday morning or another special time set aside for the festival.

In the Jewish tradition, the sabbath begins with worship at sundown on Friday and culminates with the sabbath meal on Saturday. On this Lord's day, we will combine worship and the sabbath farewell meal.

The planning committee should begin at least two months ahead making arrangements and finding leaders for preparation, activities, worship, and the congregational meal. In preparing the bulletin for the day, you will want to review the festival carefully, so that you can include the corporate readings for everyone.

Plan for a 20- to 30-minute break between the activities and the meal to set tables and put out the food for the meal. Participants will make *havdalah* candles, candleholders, spice boxes, banners, bread, and cookies for the celebration. Rather than worship in the sanctuary, the congregation will worship at the sabbath tables set up in the fellowship hall or classrooms.

As with the sabbath in a home, the atmosphere is relaxed, family and friends are gathered, the house is clean, and food is in preparation. Tables are set with simple white tablecloths, two candlesticks with new candles, two loaves of hallah, and a wine goblet filled to overflowing to represent fullness, placed near the bread. The best dishes and tableware are used. Reserve two seats at each table for the preassigned host and hostess.

You will need

□ plans for a potluck meal or a meal prepared at the church

□ leaders and materials for up to nine activity centers

□ tables and chairs and meal setup in the fellowship hall

- ❑ storytellers or strolling musicians
- ❑ a bulletin cover and the order of worship
- ❑ nametags
- ❑ enough grape juice for one brimming glass on each dinner table

- ❑ two sabbath candles for each table
- ❑ host and hostess at each table
- ❑ readers for the Invocation Litany

Name of your church

Celebrating Sabbath
Renewal of Body, Mind, and Spirit

Getting Ready

Prayers

Hymn

Activities

1. Bible Study—Look at today's scriptures and discuss sabbath.

2. *Hallah* Bread—Prepare the traditional hallah bread for the meal.

3. Manna Cookies—Make the manna cookies for the sabbath departure.

4. *Havdalah* Candle—Make candles for the sabbath tables.

5. Music—Practice hymns for worship.

6. Storytelling—Older participants prepare to tell stories about sabbath in their lives.

7. Banner/Posters—Create a banner or seven posters about creation.

8. Spice Boxes—Create something spicy and fragrant to represent sabbath renewal for the week ahead.

9. Games—Play enjoyable, quiet games.

Reenacting the Festival

Greetings

Invocation Litany

Lighting the Sabbath Candles and Unison Prayer

Hymn

Prayer of Blessing Over the Children

Scripture . . . . Proverbs 37:10, 27-30

Hymn

Kiddush

Meditation

Offering

Special Music

Blessing for the Meal

The Meal

Havdalah (the sabbath departure)
  Lighting the Havdalah Candle
  Passing the Spice Box
  Giving Out the Manna Cookies

Benediction

The Festival

Unlike manna in the wilderness, the ritual sabbath meal doesn't just appear on the table. Many people participate in getting the house and the table ready for the festival. Today, the congregation is a family celebrating the sabbath, which means that everyone helps prepare the food, the candles, the bread, and the spices that will be used at the meal. When preparations are all made, the church family will reenact a sabbath meal.

Getting Ready

When everyone has gathered, open with prayer asking the Holy Spirit to be present, renewing us and reminding us of God's saving grace. Sing a hymn if you have time. "Come, Let Us All Unite to Sing" and "Praise and Thanksgiving for Every Good Thing" are energizing gathering songs.

Before people head off to activity centers, the leader may tell briefly about *Shabbat* (pp. 83-84) and what will happen during the festival. To create a welcoming atmosphere, teach people the Hebrew words of welcome. Make a point to greet each other with these words at the activity centers and when gathering for the meal.

Shalom Aleichem: welcome

Shabbat Shalom: a good sabbath

Activities

List the choices for learning centers and their locations. Then dismiss the participants to select an activity. If there is time, they may visit more than one center.

1. Bible Study. A leader skilled in Bible study helps participants look at the scriptures for today. In addition to those listed, add Exodus 31:12-17 and Isaiah 56:6-8. Participants share how they used to observe sabbath and how they observe it now. Also look closely at Deuteronomy 5:12-15. Ask: "What new insights about sabbath do you gain from this passage?" Address questions such as:

How should we observe sabbath today?

Have we given up observing the sabbath in this culture?

Which is worse—celebrating the sabbath too much like the Pharisees, or celebrating it too little like modern Christians?

2. Hallah Bread. This group will prepare the hallah bread for the meal. Hallah is the traditional bread eaten on the sabbath. It represents the manna God provided when the Hebrews were in the wilderness. According to the story in Exodus 16, God provided bread each day, but on the sixth day there was twice as much bread, presumably to spare the Hebrews from having to gather food on the sabbath. For this reason, it is customary to serve two loaves of hallah at each table at sabbath.

You will probably want to use one of several shortcuts in order to finish baking the bread in the allotted time. Prepare any fast-rising yeast dough before the festival, and let participants shape the loaves before baking. Or use packaged bread dough from the frozen food section of your grocery. Allow plenty of time for thawing and rising before the festival. Or buy cans of crescent dinner rolls. One small can will make one braided loaf. Combine all dough from one can into a ball.

With any method, divide a softball-size lump of dough into three parts. Roll each ball between the hands until it is 9-10 inches or 20-25 centimeters long. Pinch the three ropes together at one end and braid the dough. Then pinch the loose ends together and tuck them under the loaf. Place on a cookie sheet and let rise. Bake according to package instructions until golden brown on top.

3. Manna Cookies. Make manna cookies from dough prepared ahead (recipe on p. 91) to celebrate the coming week with a renewed spirit. These will be distributed during the sabbath departure.

4. Havdalah Candle. God created light on the first day of creation. As the sabbath comes to a close and a new week begins, we light the havdalah candle in thanksgiving for God's gift of creation that began with light and the cycle that gives us a day of rest each week. The candle is braided, signifying the many religious meanings of light. God created light. Jesus Christ is the Light of the world. The Holy Spirit within us is a flame. Light also signifies hope, purification, and knowledge. This group should make one candle for each sabbath table (p. 91).

5. Music. Practice songs that will be used in the worship and prepare a special selection to sing for the congregation. "Brethren, We Have Met to Worship," "This Is the Day That the Lord Has Made," and "O God, in Restless Living" are possibilities. Also check the index of your hymnal for sabbath hymns or hymns for the Lord's Day.

6. Storytelling. Ahead of time, invite several older members of the congregation to tell stories from their lives about sabbath. How did they observe the sabbath as young people? How do they observe it now? What were they allowed to do on Sundays when they were growing up? How did they get along without malls, theaters, stereos, and television? Ask them to teach a game they may have played on Sundays. (You might suggest they share their experiences at the sabbath meal.) Let others in the group join in the storytelling after the leaders have told their stories. Allow the discussion to include sharing about when and how people of other faiths in the community observe sabbath, such as the Seventh Day Adventists, Jehovah's Witnesses, Catholics, and Jews.

7. Banner/Posters. Have this group create a banner or seven posters representing the seven days of creation. Use the colorful banner as a focal point in worship. Consider using playful symbols for the six days of creation, such as sun, waves, bugs, fish. Then say, "On the seventh day, God created rest . . . for you!"

8. Spice Boxes. When the sabbath comes to a close, the candles will be extinguished by dipping the flame into spilled grape juice that has been poured to overflowing in a goblet on the table. Then a spice box is passed around the table symbolizing the fragrance of sabbath renewal and the desire to carry the blessing of sabbath fragrance into the work of the week ahead. For churches involved in mission, this is an appropriate symbol of the cycle of work, renewal, and work.

The point of this activity is to create something fragrant and spicy. It is not necessary to make a box. Participants may (1) wrap two tablespoons of cloves or mixed whole spices in a square (4 in. or 10 cm.) of cheesecloth and tie with a ribbon; (2) punch holes in the lid of a glass jar filled with spices; (3) cover the top of a jar with netting or cheesecloth and tie the cloth in place with a ribbon around the neck of the jar; or (4) line an empty matchbox with aluminum foil, decorate the outside with brightly colored paper or felt symbols, and place whole cloves, cardamom, cinnamon sticks, or potpourri in the box.

9. Games. Since shabbat should differ from other days, we try to refrain from labor. Games that take us away from the work world and help us renew ourselves are appropriate activities for the sabbath. Avoid overly competitive or strenuous games. Younger children will like searching games such as Hide the Thimble, I Spy, Hide-and-Seek, guessing games such as Stone School, 20 Questions, or alphabet games. Others will enjoy board games, walking, playing Bible trivia games, pantomiming games, or drawing games.

Reenacting the Festival

Following the preparation activities, allow about 20-30 minutes to finalize the festival setup. Direct participants to return to the tables that have been set up in the fellowship hall or classrooms. Have children standing at the doorway, greeting people with "Shalom Aleichem" or "Good Sabbath to you." Optimally, participants of all ages should be represented at each table for discussion and activities. If participants do not know each other, the host and hostess will make introductions.

Invocation Litany

After everyone is seated, selected individuals will present the litany: "Come Let Us Go into the House of the Lord" (p. 88).

Lighting the Sabbath Candles

As the congregation reads the following prayer in unison, the hostess, representing the mother at each table, will usher in the sabbath with the kindling of the candles. She is to light the candles during the pause:

Come Let Us Go into the House of the Lord

(A: man, B: anyone, C: child, D: woman)

A:
Hurry up!

B:
Slow down.

A:
Hurry up! We'll be late again!

B:
Slow down. Remember the sabbath day to keep it holy.

All:
Lord, have mercy on us!

C:
Mom, Adam won't let me in the bathroom! He's mean!

D:
Adam, open up that door!

All:
Lord, have mercy on us.

A:
Hurry up! We'll be late for church.

B:
I was glad when they said unto me . . . Let us go into the house of the Lord.

C:
Mom, I hate this dress.

B:
Remember the sabbath day to keep it holy. Holy *(echo voice)*.

A:
We've got to go!

D:
Well, somebody has to change the baby, he's soaking wet.

A:
I have to get gas.

D:
Why in the world didn't you get it yesterday?

A:
Hey, you drive the car too!

B:
This is the day that the Lord hath made. We will rejoice and be glad in it.

All:
Lord, have mercy on us!

C:
Mom, Emily's kicking me. Make her stop.

B:
The sabbath was made for people, not people for the sabbath.

All:
Lord, have mercy on us!

A and D:
Hurry up!

B:
Be still.
Be still and know
that I am God.

All:
Lord, have mercy on us.

Come, let us welcome the sabbath. May its radiance illumine our hearts as we kindle these tapers.

Light is the symbol of the divine. The Lord is my light and my salvation.

Light is the symbol of the divine in man. The spirit of man is the light of the Lord.

Light is the symbol of the divine law. For the commandment is a lamp and the law is a light.

Light is the symbol of Israel's mission. I, the Lord, have set thee for a covenant of the people, for a light unto the nations.

Therefore, in the spirit of our ancient tradition that hallows and unites Israel in all lands and all ages, do we now kindle the sabbath lights.

(Woman lights the candles. Congregation continues.)

Blessed art Thou, O Lord our God, King of the Universe, who hast sanctified us by thy laws and commanded us to kindle the sabbath light.

May the Lord bless us with sabbath joy.

May the Lord bless us with sabbath holiness.

May the Lord bless us with sabbath peace. Amen.

Hymn

"All Things Bright and Beautiful" *or* "I Sing the Mighty Power of God" *or* "Morning Has Broken"

Prayer

The host, representing the father, recites a prayer of blessing over the children at his table, placing his hands on their heads.

Sons, God make thee as Ephraim and Manasseh.

Daughters, God make thee Sarah, Rebecca, Rachel, and Leah.

Scripture

The father then reads Proverbs 31:10, 27-30 to honor the mother.

A capable wife who can find?
She is far more precious than jewels.
She looks well to the ways of her household, and does not eat the bread of idleness.
Her children rise up and call her happy;

her husband too, and he praises her:
"Many women have done excellently,
but you surpass them all."

Charm is deceitful, and beauty is vain,
but a woman who fears the Lord is to be praised.

Hymn

"For the Beauty of the Earth" *or* "Lord of the Home"

Kiddush

The host or hostess recites the prayer of sanctification of the sabbath over a cup of wine or small individual glasses of grape juice on a tray:

Blessed art thou, O Lord our God, King of the Universe, who creates the fruit of the vine.

The host or hostess recites the blessing before the washing of hands:

Blessed art thou, O Lord Our God, King of the Universe, who has sanctified us through your commandments and us concerning the washing of hands.

Pass a covered bowl containing warm washcloths or paper towel to wipe hands.

Beginning with the father, each person in turn repeats the *Hamotzi*, a blessing over the bread:

Blessed art thou, O Lord our God, King of the Universe, who brings forth bread from the earth.

Meditation

The pastor or lay leader gives a brief meditation about sabbath. Use the following topic or write an original meditation.

We delight that Jesus caught the Pharisees in a hypocrisy. But we are just as bad about ignoring the sabbath as they were about legalizing it. We take Jesus too literally when he criticizes the Pharisees for being rigid and at the same time do nothing to commemorate the day. Today we are celebrating the sabbath, not with prescribed rituals and legalistic dedication to the law, but with joy and thanksgiving. Today we remember what God has done and take advantage of the day that was made to renew us.

Offering

Special Music
Music prepared by the music group during the activity time.

Blessing for the Meal
The host or hostess returns thanks for the meal:

Our Creator and Sustainer,

You gave us six days for laboring and one day without labor to remember you. On the sabbath we remember how we were slaves in Egypt and you delivered us. We remember how we were refugees in the wilderness and you gave us bread. We remember today that many go without bread, and we are humbled by the plentiful meal before us. Help us to use it to honor you and strengthen our bodies to do your will. Amen.

The Meal
Enjoy the meal together. As the family of God eats, the host and hostess will lead table activities.

1. Converse about how people at the table observe the sabbath. Where do they find "sabbath rest" during the week? How has the observance of sabbath changed in the years between the oldest and the youngest person at the table? Encourage older people to share the stories they told in their Storytelling Activity Center.

2. For centuries Jewish boys and girls have been given their own Bible verse that begins with the same letter as their name. Include children and adults in thinking up a passage for each person at the table. Have them write their name and verse reference on a nametag and wear it throughout the meal. See if people at the other tables know the verse without looking it up in the Bible.

3. Consider having several strolling musicians or storytellers. Storytellers can tell Bible stories or stories from the history of the congregation.

4. Allow people to converse and enjoy their meal.

Havdalah (the sabbath departure)
The host or hostess says:

[We bid] a plaintive farewell to this great day, but with zeal replenished and faith renewed. For [our] eyes are now lifted to a new shabbat, a distant yet beckoning shabbat, when life will be holy and one, humanity whole and one, and God's name perfect and one.

Lighting the Havdalah Candle
The host or hostess at each table lights the havdalah candle and recites the blessing:

Blessed art thou, O Lord, our God, Ruler of the Universe, who created the flame of the fire. Amen.

Passing the Spice Box
The host or hostess says:

The spice boxes are passed around the table so that we may inhale the fragrances, a scent that will carry us through the coming week to the next sabbath.

Giving Out the Manna Cookies
The host or hostess says:

As we depart, we pass the manna cookies, nourishment that renews us for the coming week.

Benediction
The host or hostess says:

Go now into the new week, prepared again to be servants for Christ, knowing all week long that the sabbath and our redemption is always at hand.

Extinguish the havdalah candle by dipping the flame into the spilled wine from the overflowing goblet.

Hymn
Sing "Shalom Chaverim" as a round (p. 92).

Manna Cookies

½ cup butter or margarine (125 ml)
1 cup sugar (250 ml)
2 eggs
2 tablespoons honey (30 ml)
½ teaspoon salt (2 ml)
½ teaspoon vanilla (2 ml)
1½ teaspoon baking powder (7 ml)
2 cups flour (500 ml)

Cream butter, adding sugar gradually, until light and pale. Add eggs and beat thoroughly. Add honey, salt, and vanilla. Combine baking powder with flour and add to butter mixture. Drop by half spoonsful onto greased cookie sheet. Garnish each cookie with 3 coriander seeds. Bake at 400° F or 200° C for 8 minutes or less until done. Cool on wire racks. Makes about 6 dozen cookies.

(Copyright © 1978 by Malvina Kinard and Janet Crisler. Published by Keats Publishing, Inc., New Canaan, CT, USA. Used with permission.)

Havdalah Candles

To make the candles, lay long white tapers (½" or narrower) in a flat pan filled with very hot water. When the candles are soft and pliable, twist or braid them together starting at the thick end and working toward the wicks. Make enough for at least one on a table. Extras can be used on the tables or taken home. Make candleholders from balls of modeling clay or glass jars filled with sand or fish tank gravel. Fill the jar one-third of the way with sand or gravel. Place the candle in the jar and continue filling the jar.

To avoid using hot water around young children, let them make a picture of a havdalah candle from braided crepe paper. Cut three colors of crepe paper in 12-inch or 30-centimeter strips. Staple the strips close together at the center and end of a piece of construction paper. Instruct them to cross red over green, yellow over red, green over yellow, red over green and so on until the braid nearly reaches the bottom of the paper. Draw a candle holder with crayons or cut a holder out of another color of construction paper. Cut a flame from yellow paper and glue to the top of the braid.

Shalom Chaverim

Shalom, cha-ve-rim! Shalom, cha-ve-rim! Shalom, sha-
Glad ti-dings we bring of peace on earth, good-will toward

lom! Le-hit-ra-ot, le-hit-ra-ot, Sha-lom, sha-lom.
all, Of peace on earth, of peace on earth, good-will to-ward all.

Text and Music: Israeli round

Resources

A World At Prayer: The New Ecumenical Prayer Cycle. Mystic, Conn.: Twenty-Third Publications, 1989.

Appleton, George. *Jerusalem Prayers for the World Today.* London, England: Society for Promoting Christian Knowledge, 1989.

Aschliman, Kathryn, Ed. *Growing Toward Peace.* Scottdale, Pa.: Herald Press, 1993.

Banquet of Praise: A Book of Worship Resources. Washington, D.C.: Bread for the World, 1990.

Burstein, Chaya M. *The Jewish Kids Catalog.* Philadelphia, Pa.: The Jewish Publication Society of America, 1983.

Costello, Elaine, illus. *Religious Signing.* Toronto, Ont.: Bantam Books, 1986.

DeSola, Carla. *The Spirit Moves: A Handbook of Dance and Prayer.* Austin, Tex.: The Sharing Company, 1986.

Festival: Worship with Jesus, Worship Today. Nashville, Tenn.: Cokesbury, 1992.

Fry-Miller, Kathleen; Judith Myers-Walls; and Janet Domer-Shank. *Peace Works.* Elgin, Ill.: Brethren Press, 1989.

Fry-Miller, Kathleen, and Judith Myers-Walls. *Young Peacemakers Project Book.* Elgin, Ill.: Brethren Press, 1988.

Gerber, Suella; Kathleen Jansen; and Rosemary Widner. *Becoming God's Peacemakers.* Newton, Kan.: Faith and Life Press, 1992.

In Spirit and in Truth: A Worship Book. Geneva, Switzerland: WCC Publications, 1991.

Luvmour, Sambhova and Jasette. *Everyone Wins! Cooperative Games and Activities.* Philadelphia, Pa.: New Society Publishers, 1990.

MacKenthun, Carole, and Paulinus Dwyer. *Peace.* Carthage, Ill.: Shining Star Publications, 1986.

Milen, Teddy. *Kids Who Have Made a Difference.* Northampton, Mass.: Pittenbruach Press, 1989.

Schlabach, Joetta Handrich. *Extending the Table: A World Community Cookbook.* Scottdale, Pa.: Herald Press, 1991.

Weaver, Judy. *Celebrating Holidays and Holy Days in Church and Family Settings.* Nashville, Tenn.: Discipleship Resources, 1989.

With All God's People: The New Ecumenical Prayer Cycle. Geneva, Switzerland: WCC Publications, 1989.

Zimmerman, Martha. *Celebrate the Feasts.* Minneapolis, Minn.: Bethany House, 1981.

Music

Hymnal: A Worship Book
Brethren Press
1451 Dundee Avenue
Elgin, IL 60120
800 441-3712
or
Faith & Life Press
Box 347
Newton, KS 67114-0347
800 743-2484
or
Mennonite Publishing House
616 Walnut Avenue
Scottdale, PA 15683-1999
800 245-7894

Jewish Liturgical Music
Purple Pomegranate Productions
80 Page Street
San Francisco, CA 94102

Teaching Peace (audiocassette) by Red Grammar
The Children's Bookstore Distribution
67 Wall Street, Suite 2411
New York, NY 10005

Videos

EcuFilm (an ecumenical film/video distribution service)
810 Twelfth Avenue South
Nashville, TN 37203
800 251-4091

Shalom Lifestyles (youth video curriculum)
Mennonite Media Productions
1251 Virginia Ave.
Harrisburg, VA 22801-2497
800 999-3534